Assessing Pupils' Performance Using the P Levels

Assessing Pupils' Performance Using the P Levels

DI BUCK AND VAL DAVIS

EDITED BY ANN BERGER

David Fulton Publishers

London

David Fulton Publishers Ltd
Ormond House, 26–27 Boswell Street, London WC1N 3JZ

www.fultonpublishers.co.uk

First published in Great Britain by David Fulton Publishers 2001

Note: The right of Ann Berger to be identified as the editor of this work has been asserted by her in accordance with the Copyright, Designs and Patents Act 1988.

Copyright © Bristol City Council 2001

British Library Cataloguing in Publication Data
A catalogue record for this book is available from the British Library

ISBN 1-85346-846-0

The publishers would like to thank John Cox for copyediting and proofreading this book.

Typeset by FiSH Books, London
Printed in Great Britain by Bell & Bain Ltd, Glasgow

Contents

Acknowledgements

We are indebted to the staff and pupils at the following schools:

New Fosseway School
The Florence Brown School
Kingsweston School
Briarwood School
Claremont School

Introduction

Many schools have struggled to set targets for raising achievement for pupils with learning difficulties. The QCA produced the P levels to assist with this for schools where pupils are working towards level 1 and where steps in progress are small. These P levels have just been revised and *all* schools now have a statutory obligation to set whole-school targets. These targets need to be based on an accurate assessment of what pupils know, understand and can do. This book has been written to help teachers determine accurately the level the pupils are working at. It provides work that exemplifies each P level in order that teachers can ensure that their assessments are consistent and accurate. The work in this book has been moderated across schools in Bristol to ensure accurate levels are attributed to each piece of work.

In special schools this book should be used alongside *Supporting the target setting process* published by QCA in March 2001. It will help you to ensure that targets set are based on secure assessment information. It will also help you to identify a level for pupils in the different attainment targets for English (reading and writing) and Mathematics (using and applying; number, including handling data; shape, space and measure). This information can then be used alongside *Implementing the Literacy Hour for Pupils with Learning Difficulties* (second edition) and *Implementing the National Numeracy Strategy for Pupils with Learning Difficulties* to identify the next learning objectives for pupils (both books are available from David Fulton Publishers). In mainstream schools there is increasing use of the P levels to support monitoring of progression and target setting with pupils in KS1 and with KS2 pupils with learning difficulties. Mainstream teachers will, therefore, find the book useful for accurate assessment of these pupils and in identifying future learning steps.

It is difficult to collect work from pupils at the earliest levels, as there are often no written outcomes. Much of the exemplification in this book therefore is in the form of annotated photographs. The book includes examples from special and mainstream schools and addresses the areas of reading, writing and mathematics. It is hoped that this will become a working document for schools to which teachers can add examples of their own pupils' work.

Why use this book?

The annotation sheets show three levels of attainment indicating the 'best fit' for the specific example. The level below illustrates what has preceded the current attainment level, while the level above identifies the criteria that will inform the planning for future learning steps. The elements within each level which relate to the given example are in bold type and are underlined. It should be noted that there is not an individual example for every element of every level.

The performance descriptions for P levels 1 to 3 are the same across the subjects, but with different examples to illustrate aspects of descriptions which are more context specific. There are examples of these within the book for English, Mathematics, Art and Music.

Blank copies of all the annotation sheets can be found at the back of the document and these may be photocopied for school use.

So what does the book aim to do?

- Provide clarification of the performance criteria described in *Supporting the target setting process* using illustrative examples.
- Support accurate and consistent teacher assessment of pupils working at these levels.
- Support whole-school moderation of pupils' attainment in the areas identified.
- Enable effective monitoring of attainment and progression which will support the target setting process.
- Demonstrate how assessment can be used to inform future steps in learning.

What does 'best fit' mean?

When you look at pupils' work the evidence may demonstrate elements of more than one level. It is important to consider all the criteria and make a judgement about where the performance 'best fits' the 'criteria'. The elements identified from the other levels and the gaps within the 'best fit' level will support the planning for the next steps in learning.

What is Assessment?

Assessment is one of the most powerful educational tools for promoting effective learning.

Overall the purpose of assessment is to improve standards, not merely to measure them.

(*Assessment for Learning: Beyond the Black Box*, Assessment Reform Group 1999)

Assessment is a process of gathering information which enables teachers to make judgements related to pupils' achievements in order to plan appropriately and effectively for the next steps in learning. There are different types of assessment and each serves a different and distinct purpose.

Assessment for learning (formative) is central to effective teaching and learning, happens all the time in the classroom and involves teachers and pupils. Assessment for learning shares learning objectives with pupils, provides feedback which identifies strengths and areas for development, involves pupils in self-assessment and has a commitment that every individual can improve.

Assessment of learning (summative) is carried out at the end of a unit of work, term, year, key stage or when a pupil is leaving the school in order to come to a judgement about a pupil's performance in relation to national standards – levels.

What are the purposes of Effective Assessment?

- Motivate individual learners and value their achievements.
- Find out what each pupil knows, understands and can do.
- Provide feedback which involves children in their own learning.
- Identify individual strengths and areas for development.
- Inform the planning of the next step in learning.
- Support the setting of clear targets.
- Support effective and appropriate differentiation.
- Compare pupils with national standards and expectations of progress.
- Monitor progress and enable accurate reporting upon standards attained.

Why do we need to moderate pupils' work?

- To engage in a process whereby staff share and discuss pupils' work.
- To develop a shared understanding of the assessment criteria (P levels; National Curriculum levels, etc.).
- To provide accuracy and consistency.
- To help to establish credibility in a school's ability to make accurate judgements.
- To support the monitoring role of curriculum co-ordinators.
- To provide exemplification of standards for reference.

This book will support the moderation process by providing teachers with exemplification material for the P levels and National Curriculum level 1.

What is important about moderation? Teachers become more familiar with the levels of attainment through moderation and can plan more effectively the next learning steps for pupils. They can use this process to look objectively at the outcomes of learning. In staff meetings teachers have opportunities to learn from colleagues and the process of moderation has many benefits in addition to identifying the levels of work. It enables teachers to share practice and expertise about teaching methods, planning, assessment and the curriculum.

Annotation for P levels 1 to 3

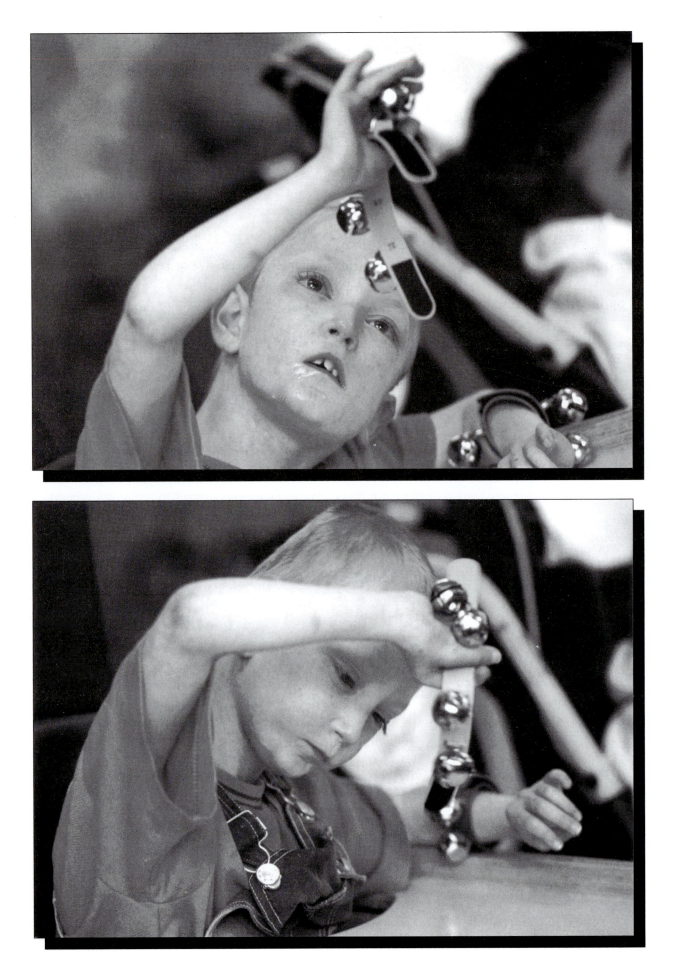

Assessing Pupils' Performance Using the P Levels

Annotation for P levels 1 to 3

Context

Music session focusing on loud/soft sounds

Evidence

Sam became very excited during the loud periods and then stilled when the instruments were played quietly.

Performance criteria

<u>P1(i)</u> <u>Pupils encounter activities and experiences.</u> They may be passive or resistant. <u>They may show simple reflex responses,</u> *for example, starting at sudden noises or movements.* <u>Any participation is fully prompted.</u>

<u>P1(ii)</u> <u>Pupils show emerging awareness of activities and experiences.</u> They may have periods when they appear alert and ready to focus their attention on certain people, events, objects or parts of objects, *for example, becoming still in a concert hall.* <u>They may give intermittent reactions,</u> *for example, sometimes becoming excited at repeated patterns of sounds.*

P2(i) Pupils begin to respond consistently to familiar people, events and objects. They react to new activities and experiences, *for example, turning towards unfamiliar sounds.* They begin to show interest in people, events and objects, *for example, smiling at a familiar person.* They accept and engage in coactive exploration, *for example, being encouraged to stroke the strings of a guitar.*

Key elements

Encounter
Emerging awareness
Intermittent reaction

Next steps

Vocalisation
Expressing likes and dislikes
Smiling, crying and other expressions of feelings

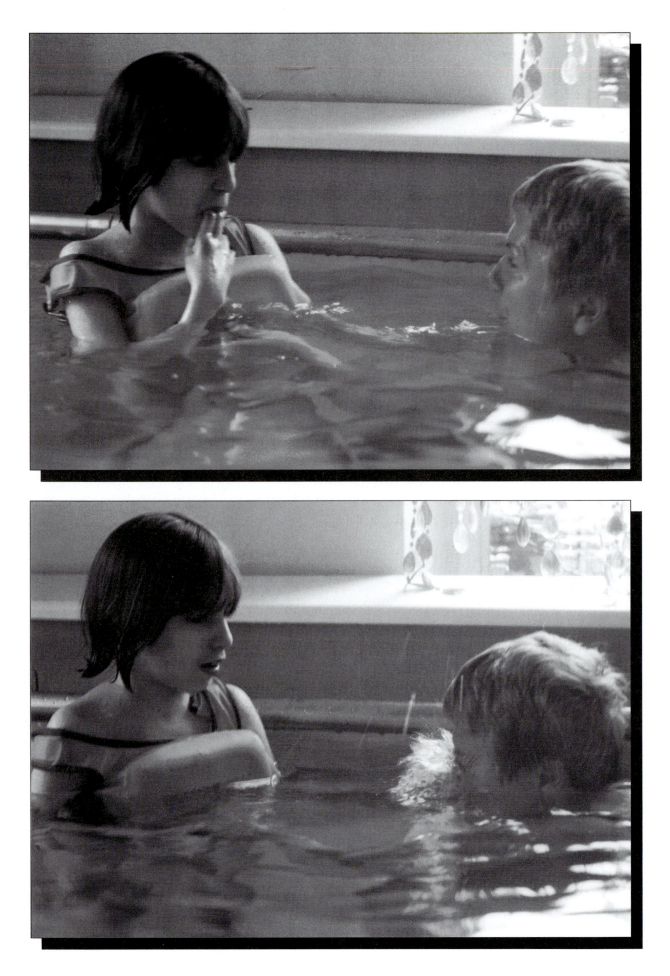

Annotation for P levels 1 to 3

Context

Communication
1:1 intensive interaction time

Comments/Evidence

While in the hydrotherapy pool Jane reached out and touched Sarah as she was blowing bubbles and making funny/silly noises and using her name.

Performance criteria

P1(i) Pupils encounter activities and experiences. They may be passive or resistant. They may show simple reflex responses, *for example, starting at sudden noises or movements.* Any participation is fully prompted.

<u>**P1(ii)** Pupils show emerging awareness of activities and experiences. They may have periods when they appear alert and ready to focus their attention on certain people,</u> events, objects or parts of objects, <u>*for example, attending briefly to interactions with a familiar person.*</u> They may give intermittent reactions, *for example, sometimes becoming excited in the midst of social activity.*

P2(i) Pupils begin to respond consistently to familiar people, events and objects. They react to new activities and experiences, *for example, withholding their attention.* They begin to show interest in people, events and objects, *for example, smiling at familiar people.* They accept and engage in coactive exploration, *for example, focusing their attention on sensory aspects of stories or rhymes when prompted.*

Key elements

Encounter
Emerging awareness
Intermittent reactions

Next steps

Awareness of objects as well as people
Visual tracking
Turning head towards person, sound

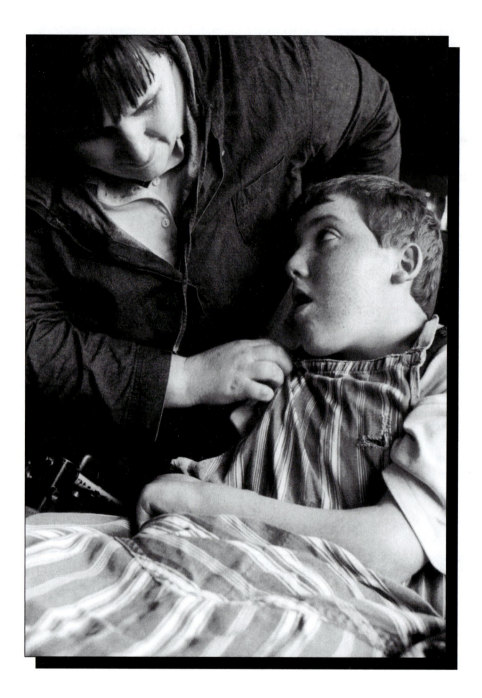

Annotation for P levels 1 to 3

Context

Communication
Getting ready for lunch

Evidence

John was sitting in the circle as the adults were putting aprons on the children for lunch. A door banged as a lunch supervisor entered the room. John jumped at the sound and began to whine and then cry.

Performance criteria

<u>**P1(i)** **Pupils encounter activities and experiences. They may be passive or resistant. They may show simple reflex responses,** *for example, starting at sudden noises or movements.* **Any participation is fully prompted.**</u>

P1(ii) Pupils show emerging awareness of activities and experiences. They may have periods when they appear alert and ready to focus their attention on certain people, events, objects or parts of objects, *for example, starting at sudden noises or movements.* They may give intermittent reactions, *for example, sometimes becoming excited in the midst of social activity.*

P2(i) Pupils begin to respond consistently to familiar people, events and objects. They react to new activities and experiences, *for example, withholding their attention.* They begin to show interest in people, events and objects, *for example, smiling at familiar people.* They accept and engage in coactive exploration, *for example, focusing their attention on sensory aspects of stories or rhymes when prompted.*

Key elements

Encounter – passive or resistant
Reactive

Next steps

Reacting with a positive response, e.g. smiling
Reacting to the same stimulus consistently

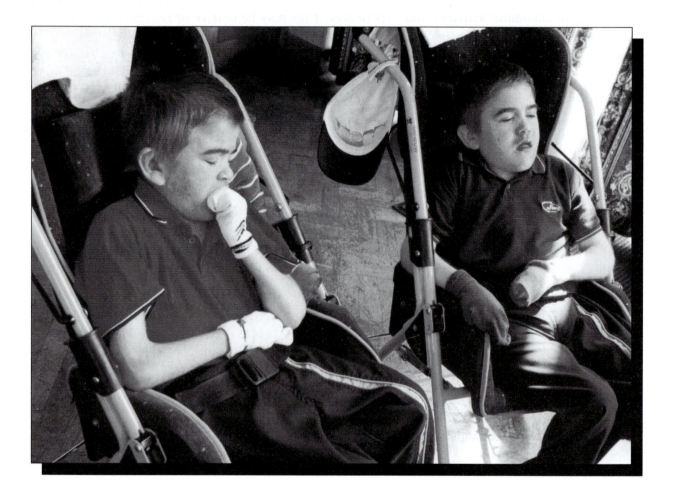

Annotation for P levels 1 to 3

Context

Communication

Evidence

During the morning 'hello' session Thomas began to smile and vocalise when adults sang to him.

Performance criteria

P1(i) Pupils encounter activities and experiences. They may be passive or resistant. They may show simple reflex responses, *for example, starting at sudden noises or movements.* Any participation is fully prompted.

P1(ii) **Pupils show emerging awareness of activities and experiences. They may have periods when they appear alert and ready to focus their attention on certain people,** events, objects or parts of objects, *for example, attending briefly to interactions with a familiar person.* **They may give intermittent reactions,** *for example, sometimes becoming excited in the midst of social activity.*

P2(i) Pupils begin to respond consistently to familiar people, events and objects. They react to new activities and experiences, *for example, withholding their attention.* They begin to show interest in people, events and objects, *for example, smiling at familiar people.* They accept and engage in coactive exploration, *for example, focusing their attention on sensory aspects of stories or rhymes when prompted.*

Key elements

Emerging awareness
Intermittent reactions

Next steps

Anticipation of routines
Turn taking
Selection of vocalisations and facial expressions
Responses to objects as well as people

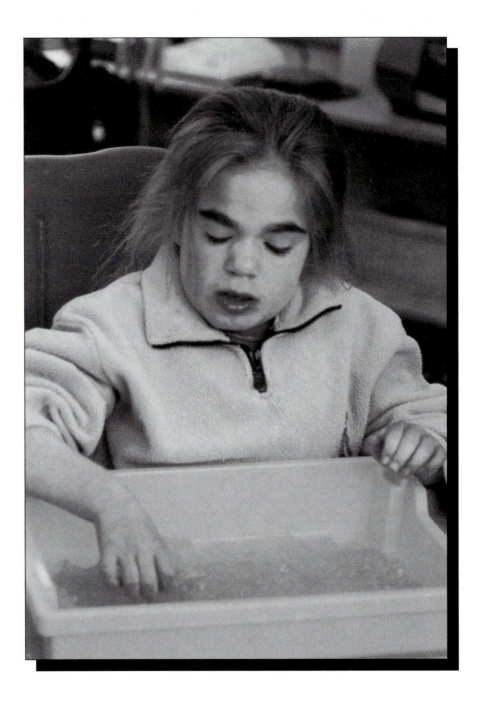

Annotation for P levels 1 to 3

Context

Group of three pupils working with two adults in an Art session

Comments/Evidence

Mary moved her hands in a bowl of jelly. She began to vocalise and showed an enjoyment of the experience.

Performance criteria

<u>P1(ii)</u> Pupils show emerging awareness of activities and experiences. They may have periods when they appear alert and ready to focus their attention on certain people, events, objects or parts of objects, *for example, looking briefly at brightly coloured objects*. They may give intermittent reactions, *for example, sometimes putting their hands in wet paint*.

P2(i) Pupils begin to respond consistently to familiar people, events and objects. <u>They react to new activities and experiences</u>, *for example, pulling their hands away from an unfamiliar texture*. <u>They begin to show interest in</u> people, <u>events and objects</u>, *for example, focusing their attention on bold black and white patterns*. <u>They accept and engage in coactive exploration</u>, *for example, feeling the textures of a range of art materials*.

<u>P2(ii)</u> Pupils begin to be proactive in their interactions. They communicate consistent preferences and affective responses, *for example, reaching for glittery materials in preference to others*. They recognise familiar people, events and objects, *for example, grasping a painting sponge*. They perform actions, often by trial and improvement, and they remember learned responses over short periods of time, *for example, returning their hands to a particular texture*. They cooperate with shared exploration and support participation, *for example, working with an adult to press, roll or pinch wet clay*.

Key elements

Awareness
Consistent response

Next steps

Using a range of toys – watching, listening, touching
Awareness of a variety of materials, e.g. cooked pasta, soapy water, shaving foam, paint

Annotation for P levels 1 to 3

Context

Number time group work. Pupils exploring bricks of different sizes and colours, independently and coatively.

Evidence

John allowed his teacher to guide his hand to the piles of bricks. He passively allowed a brick to be put into his cupped hand and looked at it. When it fell from his grasp he continued to look at it and opened his mouth in surprise.

Performance criteria

<u>P1(i)</u> **Pupils encounter activities and experiences. They may be passive or resistant**. They may show simple reflex reflex responses, *for example, starting at sudden noise or movements*. Any participation is fully prompted.

P1(ii) <u>Pupils show emerging awareness of activities and experiences. They may have periods when they appear alert and ready to focus their attention on</u> certain people, events, <u>objects or parts of objects</u>, *for example, sometimes becoming excited in the midst of a social activity.*

<u>P2(i)</u> Pupils begin to respond consistently to familiar people, events and objects. They react to new activities and experiences, *for example, withholding their attention*. They begin to show interest in people, events and objects, *for example, smiling at familiar people*. **They accept and engage in coative exploration**, *for example*, <u>focusing their attention on sensory aspects of stories or rhymes when prompted.</u>

Key elements

Emerging awareness
Responsive

Next steps

Further exploration of a variety of toys and other objects
Note responses: positive or negative

Annotation for P levels 1 to 3

Context

Sharing text in the Literacy Hour – The Gingerbread Man

Evidence

Samuel looked at the pictures as the pages were turned and responded with happy vocalisations during the repetition of phrases.

He smiled hugely when a 'real' gingerbread man was produced.

Performance criteria

P2(i) Pupils begin to respond consistently to familiar people, events and objects. They react to new activities and experiences, *for example, withholding their attention.* They begin to show interest in people, events and objects, *for example, smiling at familiar people.* They accept and engage in coactive exploration, *for example, focusing their attention on sensory aspects of stories or rhymes when prompted.*

P2(ii) Pupils begin to be proactive in their interactions. They communicate consistent preferences and affective responses, *for example, reaching out to a favourite person.* They recognise familiar people, events and objects, *for example, vocalising or gesturing in a particular way in response to a favourite visitor.* They perform actions, often by trial and improvement, and they remember learned responses over short periods of time, *for example, showing pleasure each time a particular puppet character appears in a poem dramatised with sensory cues.* They cooperate with shared exploration and support participation, *for example, taking turns in interactions with a familiar person, imitating actions and facial expressions.*

P3(i) Pupils begin to communicate intentionally. They seek attention through eye contact, gesture or action. They request events or activities, *for example, pointing to key objects or people.* They participate in shared activities with less support. They sustain concentration for periods. They explore materials in increasingly complex ways, *for example, reaching out and feeling for objects as tactile cues to events.* They observe the results of their own actions with interest, *for example, listening to their own vocalisations.* They remember learned responses over more extended periods, *for example, following the sequence of a familiar daily routine and responding appropriately.*

Key elements

Attention and response
Proactive interaction

Next steps

Expressing needs and wants as well as feelings
Anticipation of routines
Variety of vocalisations and gestures

Annotation for P levels 1 to 3

Context

Numeracy

Evidence

While on the resonance board Susan kicked her legs in order to get sensory feedback from the board. When strings of beads and blocks were placed by her feet and legs she knocked them, then stilled, then kicked again, then got excited and continued to kick faster.

Performance criteria

P2(i) Pupils begin to respond consistently to familiar people, events and objects. They react to new activities and experiences, *for example, becoming excited or alarmed when a routine is broken.* They begin to show interest in people, events and objects, *for example, tracking objects briefly across their field of awareness.* They accept and engage in coactive exploration, *for example, lifting objects briefly towards the face in shared investigations.*

P2(ii) Pupils begin to be proactive in their interactions. They communicate consistent preferences and affective responses, *for example, showing a desire to hold a favourite object.* They recognise familiar people, events and objects, *for example, looking towards their own lunch box when offered a selection.* They perform actions, often by trial and improvement, and they remember learned responses over short periods of time, for example, repeating an action with a familiar item of equipment. They cooperate with shared exploration and support participation, *for example, handling and feeling the texture of objects passed to them.*

P3(i) Pupils begin to communicate intentionally. They seek attention through eye contact, gesture or action. They request events or activities, *for example, pushing an item of equipment towards a member of staff.* They participate in shared activities with less support. They sustain concentration for periods. They explore materials in increasingly complex ways, for example, banging or rubbing objects together. They observe the results of their own actions with interest, *for example, as they throw or drop objects onto different surfaces.* They remember learned responses over more extended periods, *for example, remembering how to activate a pop-up object from a previous lesson.*

Key elements

Attention and response
Proactive interaction

Next steps

Increasingly deliberate movements
Pushing away and pulling towards self

Annotation for P levels 1 to 3

Context

Number Time: object play sessions

Evidence

Steven reached out for visually stimulating toys so that when he touched the switch music and lights are activated. He became motivated and interested by the sensory feedback. Therefore he continued to explore and manipulate the varied pieces on the toy.

Performance criteria

P2(i) Pupils begin to respond consistently to familiar people, events and objects. They react to new activities and experiences, *for example, becoming excited or alarmed when a routine is broken.* They begin to show interest in people, events and objects, *for example, tracking objects briefly across their field of awareness.* They accept and engage in coactive exploration, *for example, lifting objects briefly towards the face in shared investigations.*

P2(ii) <u>Pupils begin to be proactive in their interactions. They communicate consistent preferences and affective responses</u>, *for example, showing a desire to hold a favourite object.* They recognise familiar people, events and objects, *for example, looking towards their own lunch box when offered a selection.* <u>They perform actions, often by trial and improvement, and they remember learned responses over short periods of time,</u> *for example, repeating an action with a familiar item of equipment.* <u>They cooperate with shared exploration and support participation,</u> *for example, handling and feeling the texture of objects passed to them.*

P3(i) <u>Pupils begin to communicate intentionally.</u> They seek attention through eye contact, gesture or action. They request events or activities, *for example, pushing an item of equipment towards a member of staff.* They participate in shared activities with less support. They sustain concentration for periods. <u>They explore materials in increasingly complex ways,</u> *for example, banging or rubbing objects together.* <u>They observe the results of their own actions with interest,</u> *for example, as they throw or drop objects onto different surfaces.* They remember learned responses over more extended periods, *for example, remembering how to activate a pop-up object from a previous lesson.*

Key elements

Attention and response
Proactive interaction

Next steps

Use of a variety of toys/objects
Exploration
Object permanence
Communication of choice

Annotation for P levels 1 to 3

Context

Communication

Evidence

Nicholas sat up and responded when the home time song was played. He clearly displayed anticipation to this daily routine and enjoyed the consistency of the whole group time to end the day.

Performance criteria

P2(ii) Pupils begin to be proactive in their interactions. They communicate consistent preferences and affective responses, *for example, reaching out to a favourite person.* They recognise familiar people, events and objects, *for example, vocalising or gesturing in a particular way in response to a favourite visitor.* They perform actions, often by trial and improvement, and they remember learned responses over short periods of time, *for example, showing pleasure each time a particular puppet character appears in a poem dramatised with sensory cues.* They cooperate with shared exploration and support participation, *for example, taking turns in interactions with a familiar person, imitating actions and facial expressions.*

P3(i) <u>Pupils begin to communicate intentionally. They seek attention through eye contact, gesture or action.</u> They request events or activities, *for example, pointing to key objects or people.* <u>They participate in shared activities with less support. They sustain concentration for periods.</u> They explore materials in increasingly complex ways, *for example, reaching out and feeling for objects as tactile cues to events.* They observe the results of their own actions with interest, *for example, listening to their own vocalisations.* <u>They remember learned responses over more extended periods, *for example, following the sequence of a familiar daily routine and responding appropriately.*</u>

P3(ii) Pupils use emerging conventional communication. They greet known people and may initiate interactions and activities, *for example, prompting another person to join in with an interactive sequence.* They can remember learned responses over increasing periods of time and may anticipate known events, *for example, pre-empting sounds or actions in familiar poems.* They may respond to options and choices with actions or gestures, *for example, by nodding or shaking their heads.* They actively explore objects and events for more extended periods, *for example, turning the pages in a book shared with another person.* They apply potential solutions systematically to problems, *for example, bringing an object to an adult in order to request a new activity.*

Key elements

Engagement
Intentional communication

Next steps

Anticipation of several familiar routines
Variety of vocalisations and gestures
Eye or finger pointing

Annotation for P levels 1 to 3

Context

Communication
Group of 6 pupils with 3 adults at the table

Evidence

Sam was eating a pudding with custard when he noticed another pupil eating a banana. He gestured towards her (not quite pointing) and made loud vocalisations. It was very clear that he wanted the banana. He smiled when given a piece of banana, ate it, and gestured for more.

Performance criteria

P2(ii) Pupils begin to be proactive in their interactions. They communicate consistent preferences and affective responses, *for example, reaching out to a favourite person*. They recognise familiar people, events and objects, *for example, vocalising or gesturing in a particular way in response to a favourite visitor*. They perform actions, often by trial and improvement, and they remember learned responses over short periods of time, *for example, showing pleasure each time a particular puppet character appears in a poem dramatised with sensory cues*. They cooperate with shared exploration and support participation, *for example, taking turns in interactions with a familiar person, imitating actions and facial expressions*.

P3(i) <u>Pupils begin to communicate intentionally. They seek attention through eye contact, gesture or action. They request events or activities,</u> *for example, pointing to key objects or people*. <u>They participate in shared activities with less support. They sustain concentration for periods.</u> They explore materials in increasingly complex ways, *for example, reaching out and feeling for objects as tactile cues to events*. <u>They observe the results of their own actions</u> with interest, *for example, listening to their own vocalisations*. They remember learned responses over more extended periods, *for example, following the sequence of a familiar daily routine and responding appropriately*.

P3(ii) <u>Pupils use emerging conventional communication.</u> They greet known people and may initiate interactions and activities, *for example, prompting another person to join in with an interactive sequence*. They can remember learned responses over increasing periods of time and may anticipate known events, *for example, pre-empting sounds or actions in familiar poems*. They may respond to options and choices with actions or gestures, *for example, by nodding or shaking their heads*. They actively explore objects and events for more extended periods, *for example, turning the pages in a book shared with another person*. They apply potential solutions systematically to problems, *for example, bringing an object to an adult in order to request a new activity*.

Key elements

Attention and reponse
Engagement
Emerging conventional communication

Next steps

Showing preferences for objects – other than food
More vocalisation

Annotation for P levels 1 to 3

Context

Communication

Evidence

When offered fruit and biscuits, Nicholas chose the fruit above the biscuits. He made this choice by reaching for the plate and by facial expression when given a biscuit instead of the fruit. When given fruit he ate it, when given a biscuit he spat it out and reached for the fruit.

Performance criteria

P2(ii) Pupils begin to be proactive in their interactions. They communicate consistent preferences and affective responses, *for example, reaching out to a favourite person.* They recognise familiar people, events and objects, *for example, vocalising or gesturing in a particular way in response to a favourite visitor.* They perform actions, often by trial and improvement, and they remember learned responses over short periods of time, *for example, showing pleasure each time a particular puppet character appears in a poem dramatised with sensory cues.* They cooperate with shared exploration and support participation, *for example, taking turns in interactions with a familiar person, imitating actions and facial expressions.*

P3(i) Pupils begin to communicate intentionally. They seek attention through eye contact, gesture or action. They request events or activities, *for example, pointing to key objects or people.* They participate in shared activities with less support. They sustain concentration for periods. They explore materials in increasingly complex ways, *for example, reaching out and feeling for objects as tactile cues to events.* They observe the results of their own actions with interest, *for example, listening to their own vocalisations.* They remember learned responses over more extended periods, *for example, following the sequence of a familiar daily routine and responding appropriately.*

P3(ii) Pupils use emerging conventional communication. They greet known people and may initiate interactions and activities, *for example, prompting another person to join in with an interactive sequence.* They can remember learned responses over increasing periods of time and may anticipate known events, *for example, pre-empting sounds or actions in familiar poems.* They may respond to options and choices with actions or gestures, *for example, by nodding or shaking their heads.* They actively explore objects and events for more extended periods, *for example, turning the pages in a book shared with another person.* They apply potential solutions systematically to problems, *for example, bringing an object to an adult in order to request a new activity.*

Key elements

Engagement
Emerging conventional communication

Next steps

Reaching out for objects and toys
Manipulating objects and toys
Making definite choices
Showing greater interest in routines and objects

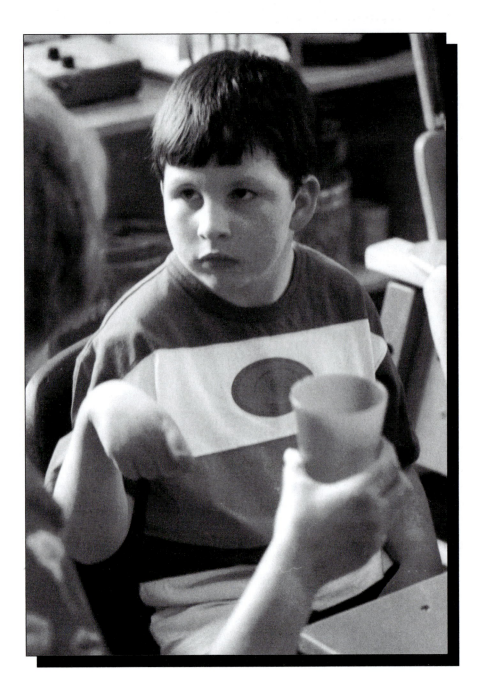

Annotation for P levels 1 to 3

Context

Communication

Evidence

James signed 'yes' and vocalised for a drink at drinks time.
He looked at an adult, smiled and vocalised to indicate that he wanted a drink.

Performance criteria

<u>P2(ii)</u> Pupils begin to be proactive in their interactions. They communicate consistent preferences and affective responses, *for example, reaching out to a favourite person.* They recognise familiar people, events and objects, *for example, vocalising or gesturing in a particular way in response to a favourite visitor.* They perform actions, often by trial and improvement, and they remember learned responses over short periods of time, *for example, showing pleasure each time a particular puppet character appears in a poem dramatised with sensory cues.* They cooperate with shared exploration and support participation, *for example, taking turns in interactions with a familiar person, imitating actions and facial expressions.*

<u>P3(i)</u> Pupils begin to communicate intentionally. They seek attention through eye contact, gesture or action. They request events or activities, *for example, pointing to key objects or people.* They participate in shared activities with less support. They sustain concentration for periods. They explore materials in increasingly complex ways, *for example, reaching out and feeling for objects as tactile cues to events.* They observe the results of their own actions with interest, *for example, listening to their own vocalisations.* They remember learned responses over more extended periods, *for example, following the sequence of a familiar daily routine and responding appropriately.*

<u>P3(ii)</u> <u>Pupils use emerging conventional communication. They greet known people and may initiate interactions and activities,</u> <u>*for example, prompting another person to join in with an interactive sequence.*</u> <u>They can remember learned responses over increasing periods of time and may anticipate known events,</u> *for example, pre-empting sounds or actions in familiar poems.* <u>They may respond to options and choices with actions or gestures,</u> <u>*for example, by nodding or shaking their heads.*</u> They actively explore objects and events for more extended periods, *for example, turning the pages in a book shared with another person.* They apply potential solutions systematically to problems, *for example, bringing an object to an adult in order to request a new activity.*

Key elements

Engagement
Emerging conventional communication

Next steps

Repeating words
Developing a vocabulary of single words
Vocalising and gesturing together

Language and Literacy: Reading

Assessing Pupils' Performance Using the P Levels

Language and Literacy: Reading

Annotation for P levels 3, 4 and 5

Context

Sharing a book with another child

Evidence

Ruth chose a book from the shelf by pointing. She held the book correctly and began to turn the pages. She vocalised as she looked at each page and occasionally pushed the book towards another child. She pointed to the pictures and vocalised but used no recognisable words. When she had finished she shouted to attract attention and pointed to the shelf for another book.

Performance criteria – Reading

P3(ii) Pupils use emerging conventional communication. They greet known people and may initiate interactions and activities, *for example, prompting another person to join in with an interactive sequence.* They can remember learned responses over increasing periods of time and may anticipate known events, *for example, pre-empting sounds or actions in familiar poems.* They may respond to options and choices with actions or gestures, *for example, by nodding or shaking their heads.* They actively explore objects and events for more extended periods, *for example, turning the pages in a book shared with another person.* They apply potential solutions to problems, *for example, bringing an object to an adult in order to request a new activity.*

P4 Pupils listen and respond to familiar rhymes and stories. They show some understanding of how books work, *for example, turning pages and holding the book the right way up.*

P5 Pupils select a few words, signs or symbols with which they are particularly familiar and derive some meaning from text, symbols or signs presented in a way familiar to them. They show curiosity about content at a simple level, *for example, they may answer basic two-word questions about the story.* They match objects to pictures and symbols.

Key elements

From object to picture
Representation awareness, e.g., recognition that pictures can represent objects/people

Next steps

'Show me the.......'
'Find the book about.......'
Interpreting and using signs related to stories

Language and Literacy: Reading

Annotation for P levels 3, 4 and 5

Context

Sharing a book with a teacher

Evidence

Graham looked at the picture on the cover and said, 'Animals'. He opened the book and found the first page, looking first at the left hand page and then at the right hand page. He occasionally said the name of the animals in the photograph and spent time looking at each picture. He made no attempt to point to the text at the bottom of the page.

Performance criteria – Reading

P3(ii) Pupils use emerging conventional communication. They greet known people and may initiate interactions and activities, *for example, prompting another person to join in with an interactive sequence.* They can remember learned responses over increasing periods of time and may anticipate known events, *for example, pre-empting sounds or actions in familiar poems.* They may respond to options and choices with actions or gestures, *for example, by nodding or shaking their heads.* They actively explore objects and events for more extended periods, *for example, turning the pages in a book shared with another person.* They apply potential solutions to problems, *for example, bringing an object to an adult in order to request a new activity.*

P4 Pupils listen and respond to familiar rhymes and stories. They show some understanding of how books work, *for example, turning pages and holding the book the right way up.*

P5 Pupils select a few words, signs or symbols with which they are particularly familiar and derive some meaning from text, symbols or signs presented in a way familiar to them. They show curiosity about content at a simple level, *for example, they may answer basic two-word questions about the story.* They match objects to pictures and symbols.

Key elements

From object to picture
Recognition that pictures represent objects/people

Next steps

Answer questions about pictures
Teacher to read while running finger under text

Assessing Pupils' Performance Using the P Levels

Language and Literacy: Reading

Annotation for P levels 3, 4 and 5

Context

Individual pupil sharing a book with an adult

Evidence

Max held the book the right way up and turned the pages appropriately. He focused on the left hand page, ignoring the right hand page altogether. He pointed to the text on each page saying 'Lee', but pointing to 'Look'. He said 'all gone' at the last page. He didn't comment on any of the pictures.

Performance criteria – Reading

P3(ii) Pupils use emerging conventional communication. They greet known people and may initiate interactions and activities, *for example, prompting another person to join in with an interactive sequence.* They can remember learned responses over increasing periods of time and may anticipate known events, *for example, pre-empting sounds or actions in familiar poems.* They may respond to options and choices with actions or gestures, *for example, by nodding or shaking their heads.* They actively explore objects and events for more extended periods, *for example, turning the pages in a book shared with another person.* They apply potential solutions to problems, *for example, bringing an object to an adult in order to request a new activity.*

P4 Pupils listen and respond to familiar rhymes and stories. They show some understanding of how books work, *for example, turning pages and holding the book the right way up.*

P5 Pupils select a few words, signs or symbols with which they are particularly familiar and derive some meaning from text, symbols or signs presented in a way familiar to them. They show curiosity about content at a simple level, *for example, they may answer basic two-word questions about the story.* They match objects to pictures and symbols.

Key elements

Picture to symbol
Abstract representation – may recognise own name

Next steps

Respond to questions about content (picture)
Matching objects to symbols

Language and Literacy: Reading

Annotation for P levels 4, 5 and 6

Context

Planning: choice of activities

Evidence

Victoria pointed to her name on the planning board and put the symbol of the activity she wanted to do next to her name. She clearly understood what the activity was.

Performance criteria – Reading

P4 Pupils listen and respond to familiar rhymes and stories. They show some understanding of how books work, *for example, turning pages and holding the book the right way up.*

<u>P5 Pupils select a few words, signs or symbols with which they are particularly familiar</u> and <u>derive some meaning from text, symbols or signs presented in a way familiar to them. They show curiosity about content at a simple level,</u> *for example, they may answer basic two-word questions about the story.* They match objects to pictures and symbols.

<u>P6 Pupils select and recognise or read a small number of words or symbols linked to a familiar vocabulary, for example, name,</u> people, objects or actions. They match letters and short words.

Key elements

Picture to symbol
More abstract representation
May select own name

Next steps

Select single words from print
Use initial letter cards
Develop simple sight vocabulary

Language and Literacy: Reading

Annotation for P levels 6, 7 and 8

Context

Reading a book called 'Who built the ark?' The class had previously read the book during the Literacy Hour.

Evidence

Leon opened the book and pointed to the text. He anticipated what was written based on his memory of the text saying, 'Look at the monkeys', 'Look at the lions'. He pointed left to right along the line of text. He turned each page and looked at the left side first. He looked at each picture knowing that the text related to the picture.

Performance criteria – Reading

P6 Pupils select and recognise or read a small number of words or symbols linked to a familiar vocabulary, for example, name, people, objects or actions. They match letters and short words.

P7 <u>Pupils show an interest in the activity of reading. They predict words</u>, signs or symbols <u>in narrative</u>, for example when the adult stops reading, pupils fill in the missing word. <u>They distinguish between print and pictures in texts. They understand the conventions of presentation in their preferred mode of communication, for example, left to right orientation, top to bottom, page following page.</u> They can recognise some letters of the alphabet.

P8 <u>Pupils understand that words, signs, symbols and pictures convey meaning.</u> They read or recognise a growing repertoire of familiar words or symbols, including their own names. They recognise letters of the alphabet by shape, name and sound. They begin to associate sounds with patterns in rhymes, with syllables, and with words, signs, symbols and letters.

Key elements

Informed 'guessing'
Exploring sounds

Next steps

Using initial letters

Language and Literacy: Reading

Annotation for P levels 6, 7 and 8

Context

Shared text and shared word work during the Literacy Hour

Evidence

John matched initial letter sounds to pictures. He vocalised each sound and the word. He is beginning to associate a picture with some letters of the alphabet. He can name the picture when shown a letter and pick out a picture when told its initial sound. He can supply initial phoneme, e.g., 'Pirate..., P...P...P...'. He can follow text left to right matching voice to print.

Performance criteria – Reading

P6 Pupils select and recognise or read a small number of words or symbols linked to a familiar vocabulary, for example, name, people, objects or actions. They match letters and short words.

P7 Pupils show an interest in the activity of reading. They predict words, signs or symbols in narrative, for example, when the adult stops reading, pupils fill in the missing word. They distinguish between print and pictures in texts. They understand the conventions of presentation in their preferred mode of communication, for example, left to right orientation, top to bottom, page following page. They can recognise some letters of the alphabet.

P8 Pupils understand that words, signs, symbols and pictures convey meaning. They read or recognise a growing repertoire of familiar words or symbols, including their own names. They recognise letters of the alphabet by shape, name and sound. They begin to associate sounds with patterns in rhymes, with syllables, and with words, signs, symbols and letters.

Key elements

Playing with words
Exploring sound and patterns of sound

Next steps

Recognise letters by shape and sound
Exploring sound and patterns of sound

Language and Literacy: Reading

Annotation for P level 8 and National Curriculum levels 1C and 1B

Context

Pupil reads from a book of her choice to an adult

Evidence

Linda took the book and pointed to the words. She turned pages appropriately and read along the line of print from left to right, pointing to each word and matching voice to print.
She hesitated over words which she did not use spontaneously in speech.

Performance criteria – Reading

P8 Pupils understand that words, signs, symbols and pictures convey meaning. They read or recognise a growing repertoire of familiar words or symbols, including their own names. They recognise letters of the alphabet by shape, name and sound. They begin to associate sounds with patterns in rhymes, with syllables, and with words, signs, symbols and letters.

1C <u>Pupils can recognise familiar words, signs or symbols in simple texts. They identify initial sounds in unfamiliar words. They can establish meaning when reading aloud simple sentences, sometimes with prompting.</u> They express their response to familiar texts by identifying aspects which they like and dislike.

1B <u>Pupils can read a range of familiar words</u>, signs or symbols and identify initial and final sounds in unfamiliar words. With support they use their knowledge of letters, sounds and words to establish meaning when reading aloud. They respond to events and ideas in poems, stories and non-fiction.

Next steps

Increase range of familiar words
Use familiar words to develop knowledge of letters and sounds
Provide opportunities for talk in response to stories and poems

Language and Literacy: Writing

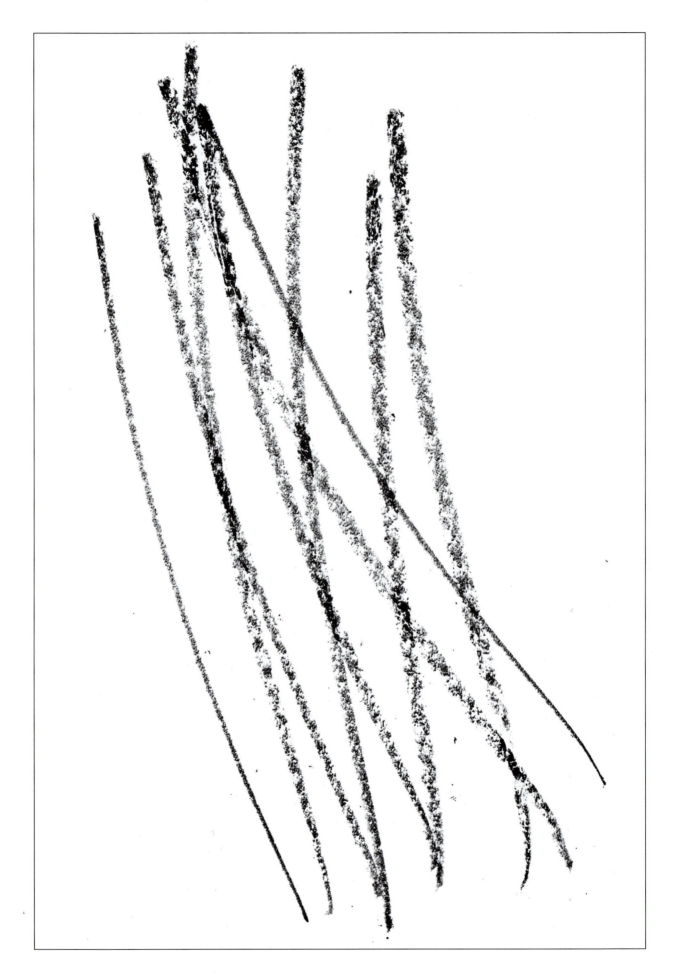

Language and Literacy: Writing

Annotation for P levels 3, 4 and 5

Context

Choosing and using crayons
Position supported in a standing frame

Evidence

Rosie chose the colour crayons to be put in her box. She used quite deliberate strokes of the crayon across the piece of paper from left to right. She held the crayon in her left hand and varied her grip throughout but maintained her obvious enjoyment and enthusiasm for approximately ten minutes. She constantly looked down at her work and took great pride in the result.

Performance criteria – Writing

P3(ii) Pupils use emerging conventional communication. They greet known people and may initiate interactions and activities, *for example, prompting another person to join in with an interactive sequence.* They can remember learned responses over increasing periods of time and may anticipate known events, *for example, pre-empting sounds or actions in familiar poems.* They may respond to options and choices with actions or gestures, *for example, by nodding or shaking their heads.* They actively explore objects and events for more extended periods, *for example, turning the pages in a book shared with another person.* They apply potential solutions systematically to problems, *for example, bringing an object to an adult in order to request a new activity.*

P4 Pupils begin to understand that marks and symbols convey meaning, for example, scribbling alongside a picture or placing photographs or symbols on a personal timetable. <u>They make marks or symbols in their preferred mode of communication</u>, *for example, using writing implements with a pincer grip, generating a symbol from a selection on a computer.*

P5 Pupils produce some meaningful print, signs or symbols associated with their own name or familiar spoken words, actions, images or events, *for example, contributing to records of their own achievements or to books about themselves, their families and interests.* They trace, overwrite and copy under or over a model, making horizontal, vertical and circular lines. With support, they make and complete patterns.

Key elements

Range of mark making

Next steps

Developing a variety of mark making movements, e.g. circles; up and down; round the edge

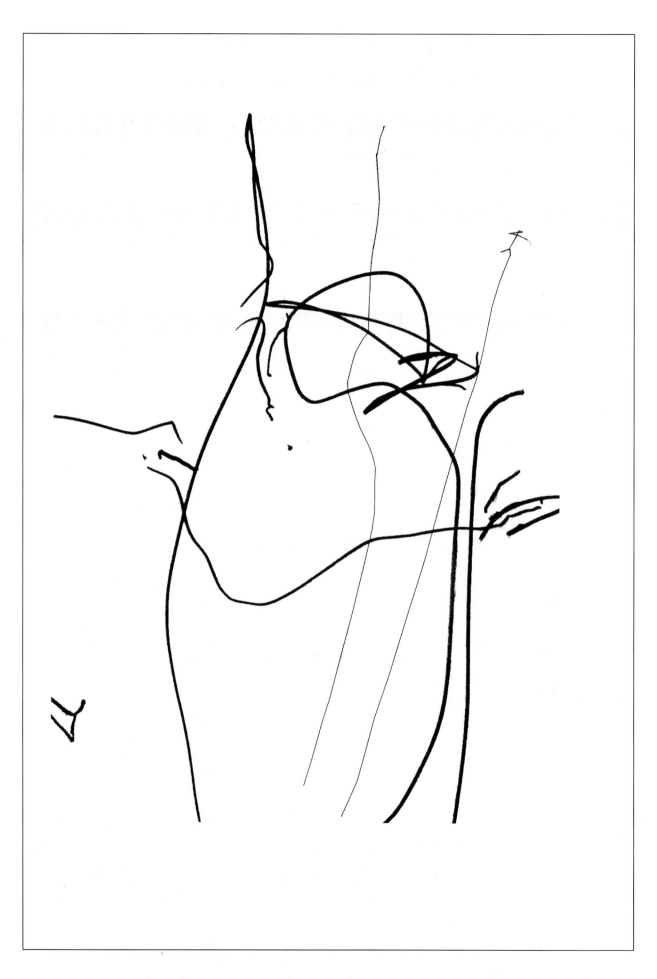

Language and Literacy: Writing

Annotation for P levels 3, 4 and 5

Context

Writing session following role play activity in the Home corner where children had been pretending they were in a café

Evidence

Danny was the waiter and was writing down the 'order' for 'customers' in the café. At one point he discarded the pencil he was using in favour of a pen and appeared pleased with the results.

Performance criteria – Writing

P3(ii) Pupils use emerging conventional communication. They greet known people and may initiate interactions and activities, *for example, prompting another person to join in with an interactive sequence.* They can remember learned responses over increasing periods of time and may anticipate known events, *for example, pre-empting sounds or actions in familiar poems.* They may respond to options and choices with actions or gestures, *for example, by nodding or shaking their heads.* They actively explore objects and events for more extended periods, *for example, turning the pages in a book shared with another person.* They apply potential solutions to problems systematically, *for example, bringing an object to an adult in order to request a new activity.*

P4 <u>Pupils begin to understand that marks and symbols convey meaning</u>, *for example, scribbling alongside a picture or placing photographs or symbols on a personal timetable.* <u>They make marks or symbols in their preferred mode of communication, for example, using writing implements with a pincer grip</u>, generating a symbol from a selection on a computer.

P5 Pupils produce some meaningful print, signs or symbols associated with their own name or familiar spoken words, actions, images or events, *for example, contributing to records of their own achievements or to books about themselves, their families and interests.* They trace, overwrite and copy under or over a model, making horizontal, vertical and circular lines. With support, they make and complete patterns.

Key elements

Range of mark making

Next steps

Developing a variety of mark making movements, e.g. circles; up and down

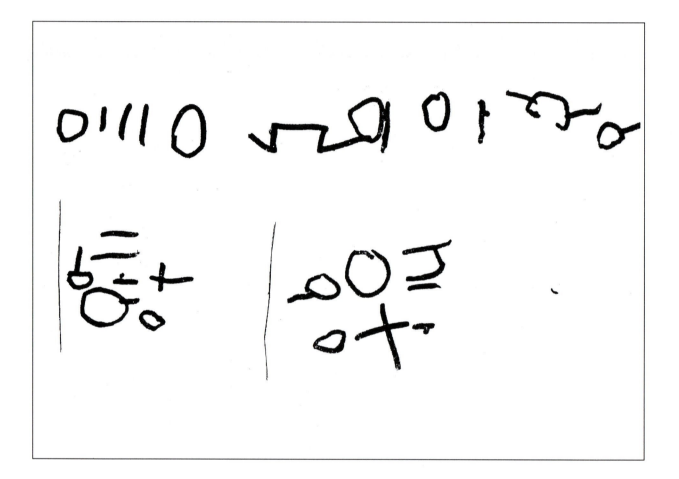

Language and Literacy: Writing

Annotation for P levels 3, 4 and 5

Context

Copying magnetic letters

Evidence

Michael was interested in the magnetic letters. He arranged them on a magnetic board and copied letters from the board.

He is showing some knowledge about the letters in his name – picked W for M.

Performance criteria – Writing

P3(ii) Pupils use emerging conventional communication. They greet known people and may initiate interactions and activities, *for example, prompting another person to join in with an interactive sequence.* They can remember learned responses over increasing periods of time and may anticipate known events, *for example, pre-empting sounds or actions in familiar poems.* They may respond to options and choices with actions or gestures, *for example, by nodding or shaking their heads.* They actively explore objects and events for more extended periods, *for example, turning the pages in a book shared with another person.* They apply potential solutions to problems systematically, *for example, bringing an object to an adult in order to request a new activity.*

P4 Pupils begin to understand that marks and symbols convey meaning, *for example, scribbling alongside a picture or placing photographs or symbols on a personal timetable.* They make marks or symbols in their preferred mode of communication, *for example, using writing implements with a pincer grip,* *generating a symbol from a selection on a computer.*

P5 Pupils produce some meaningful print, signs or symbols associated with their own name or familiar spoken words, actions, images or events, *for example contributing to records of their own achievements or to books about themselves, their families and interests.* They trace, overwrite and copy under or over a model, making horizontal, vertical and circular lines. With support, they make and complete patterns.

Key elements

Range of mark making
Communicating meaning through emergent writing

Next steps

Sequence and trace the letters of name
Matching to words (and pictures)
Focusing on the initial letters of written words (highlighting, alliterative sentences, sorting words and pictures)

zheijookkkkkyieshgggggggggggggggggunnnnnnygtrfb4rfrc

Language and Literacy: Writing

Annotation for P levels 4, 5 and 6

Context

Using a computer and word processor after a lesson focusing on the names of the pupils in the class

Evidence

Zheta typed a long series of lower case letters beginning with the first three letters of her own name and including the initial letters of several other pupils in the class – James, Katie, George

Performance criteria – Writing

P4 Pupils begin to understand that marks and symbols convey meaning, *for example, scribbling alongside a picture or placing photographs or symbols on a personal timetable.* They make marks or symbols in their preferred mode of communication, *for example, using writing implements with a pincer grip, generating a symbol from a selection on a computer.*

P5 Pupils produce some meaningful print, signs or symbols associated with their own name or familiar spoken words, actions, images or events, *for example, contributing to records of their own achievements or to books about themselves, their families and interests.* They trace, overwrite and copy under or over a model, making horizontal, vertical and circular lines. With support, they make and complete patterns.

P6 Pupils differentiate between letters and symbols, *for example, producing a drawing to accompany writing.* They copy writing with support, *for example, labels and/or captions for pictures or for displays.*
They produce or write recognisable letters or symbols related to their names.

Key elements

Letter-like shapes
Emergent writing, self initiated, may say what the writing means, defining writing as opposed to pictures

Next steps

Copying over and under a variety of familiar words
Attempt to write words, e.g. shopping list; my family

Language and Literacy: Writing

Annotation for P levels 5, 6 and 7

Context

Singing the song 1, 2, 3, 4, 5 . . . . . . Once I caught a fish alive
Looking at pictures of creatures found by the sea

Evidence

Jordan drew a picture and wrote some letters. The teacher asked him to point to his writing which Jordan did. When he was asked 'What does your writing say?' Jordan answered 'The crab is eating my finger.'

Performance criteria – Writing

P5 Pupils produce some meaningful print, signs or symbols associated with their own name or familiar spoken words, **actions, images or events,** *for example, contributing to records of their own achievements or to books about themselves, their families and interests.* **They** trace, overwrite and **copy under or over a model,** making horizontal, vertical and circular lines. With support, they make and complete patterns.

P6 Pupils differentiate between letters and symbols, *for example, producing a drawing to accompany writing.* They copy writing with support, *for example, labels and/or captions for pictures or for displays.*
They produce or write recognisable letters or symbols related to their names.

P7 Pupils group letters and leave spaces between them as though they are writing separate words. Some letters are correctly formed. They are aware of the sequence of letters, symbols and words, *for example, selecting and linking symbols together, writing their own names and one or two other simple words from memory.*

Key elements

No evidence of differentiation between symbols and letters

Next steps

Recognising letters
Handwriting skills in letter formation
Extending length of writing

Language and Literacy: Writing

Annotation for P levels 5, 6 and 7

Context

Pupils had enjoyed a speaking and listening session talking about holidays

Evidence

James drew his family and wrote about his recent holiday. He could say precisely what his writing said.

Performance criteria – Writing

P5 Pupils produce some meaningful print, signs or symbols associated with their own name or familiar spoken words, actions, images or events, *for example, contributing to records of their own achievements or to books about themselves, their families and interests.* They trace, overwrite and copy under or over a model, making horizontal, vertical and circular lines. With support, they make and complete patterns.

P6 Pupils differentiate between letters and symbols, *for example, producing a drawing to accompany writing.* They copy writing with support, *for example, labels and/or captions for pictures or for displays.*
They produce or write recognisable letters or symbols related to their names.

P7 Pupils group letters and leave spaces between them as though they are writing separate words. Some letters are correctly formed. They are aware of the sequence of letters, symbols and words, *for example, selecting and linking symbols together, writing their own names and one or two other simple words from memory.*

Key elements

Sequencing
Understanding of left – right
Words/groups of letters

Next steps

Using initial letters accurately
Developing a small bank of words relating to familiar people, objects, events, to be used independently

Language and Literacy: Writing

Annotation for P levels 7 and 8 and National Curriculum level 1C

Context

There was a class discussion about families. Pupils were asked to draw a picture of their family.

Evidence

Rebecca wrote her name independently and used the initial letter for Mummy, Daddy, Fred and Linda.

Performance criteria – Writing

<u>**P7**</u> Pupils group letters and leave spaces between them as though they are writing separate words. <u>**Some letters are correctly formed. They are aware of the sequence of letters, symbols and words,**</u> *<u>for example, selecting and linking symbols together, writing their own names</u>* and *one or two other simple words from memory.*

<u>**P8**</u> <u>**In their writing and recording pupils use pictures, symbols and familiar words and letters to communicate meaning,**</u> showing awareness of the different purposes, *for example, letters, lists, stories or instructions of writing.* They write their names with appropriate use of upper and lower case letters or appropriate symbols.

1C Pupils produce recognisable letters and symbols to convey meaning.
Some commonly used letters are correctly shaped but may still be inconsistent in size and orientation.
Some of their writing may still need to be mediated to be understood.

Key elements

Sequencing
Words/groups of letters

Next steps

Developing independent use of word bank of familiar words

Dear Miss

A S a L K S [S i n t r a i n

likes

racing

train (found in Picture Dictionary

i L C t u g b o a t q h t

(picture dictionary)

I   like

I

hate

W r d s

Words.

L V f c o m ñ s a

love

Language and Literacy: Writing

Annotation for P levels 7 and 8 and National Curriculum level 1C

Context

In this class the teacher was ill and away from school, so the supply teacher asked the pupils to write her a letter to cheer her up

Evidence

Asa told his teacher what it was that he wanted to write and he then attempted words, with the teacher articulating the words slowly and clearly several times.
He is beginning to segment single words on request, but not in this case, i.e. in order to write.

Performance criteria – Writing

<u>P7</u> <u>Pupils group letters and leave spaces between them as though they are writing separate words. Some letters are correctly formed. They are aware of the sequence of letters, symbols and words,</u> *for example, selecting and linking symbols together, writing their own names and one or two other simple words from memory.*

<u>P8</u> <u>In their writing and recording pupils use pictures, symbols and familiar words and letters to communicate meaning,</u> showing awareness of the different purposes, *for example, letters, lists, stories or instructions of writing.* <u>They write their names with appropriate use of upper and lower case letters</u> or appropriate symbols.

<u>1C</u> <u>Pupils produce recognisable letters and symbols to convey meaning.</u>
<u>Some commonly used letters are correctly shaped but may still be inconsistent in size and orientation.</u>
Some of their writing may still need to be mediated to be understood.

Key elements

Random letters
Groups of letters/words

Next steps

Building on phonic knowledge
Use of medial vowel sounds
Learning to leave spaces between words

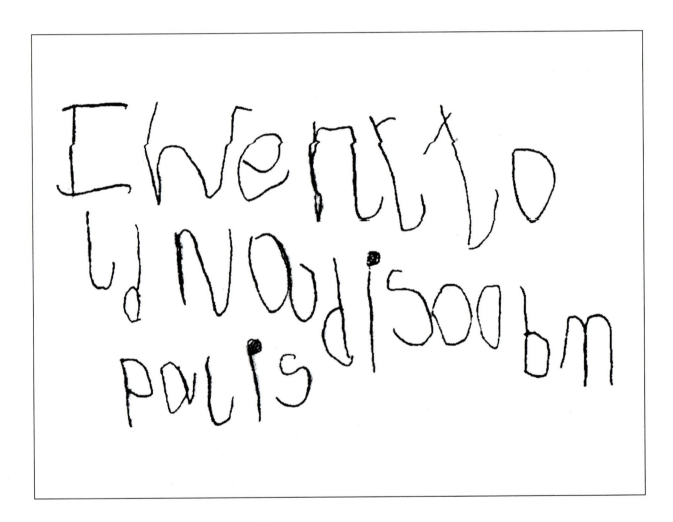

Language and Literacy: Writing

Annotation for P levels 7 and 8 and National Curriculum level 1C

Context

Journal writing session in class where the task was to recall a recent event

Evidence

Susan produced this piece of independent writing using some invented spelling. When asked what she had written she replied, 'I went to London and I saw Buckingham Palace.'

Performance criteria – Writing

P7 Pupils group letters and leave spaces between them as though they are writing separate words. Some letters are correctly formed. They are aware of the sequence of letters, symbols and words, *for example, selecting and linking symbols together, writing their own names and one or two other simple words from memory.*

P8 In their writing and recording pupils use pictures, symbols and familiar words and letters to communicate meaning, showing awareness of the different purposes, *for example, letters, lists, stories or instructions of writing.* They write their names with appropriate use of upper and lower case letters or appropriate symbols.

1C Pupils produce recognisable letters and symbols to convey meaning. Some commonly used letters are correctly shaped but may still be inconsistent in size and orientation. Some of their writing may still need to be mediated to be understood.

Key elements

Groups of letters/words

Next steps

Leaving finger spaces
Working on full stops
Using a word book

Friday 2 May

I have a wit ca~.
and I have a bulic dcc.
I run fus wen Im hye I run.
uret it? i am or get. I have sip.
on mi tac I have Sab on.
mital. Wo am I Ia def.

Language and Literacy: Writing

Annotation for P level 8 and National Curriculum levels 1C and 1B

Context

Writing in response to book 'Big and Bulky'

Evidence

Karen has written in response using some elements of the book's structure. Her writing communicates some phrases of coherent meaning to an outside reader.

Performance criteria – Writing

P8 In their writing and recording pupils use pictures, symbols and familiar words and letters to communicate meaning, showing awareness of the different purposes, *for example, letters, lists, stories or instructions of writing.* They write their names with appropriate use of upper and lower case letters or appropriate symbols.

1C <u>Pupils produce recognisable letters and symbols to convey meaning.</u>
<u>Some commonly used letters are correctly shaped but may still be inconsistent in size and orientation.</u>
<u>Some of their writing may still need to be mediated to be understood.</u>

1B <u>Pupils structure some phrases and simple statements using recognisable words to communicate ideas.</u>
Their writing can generally be understood without mediation.
They begin to show an understanding of how full stops are used. Most letters are clearly shaped and correctly orientated.

Key elements

Capital letters generally correctly used

Next steps

Letter construction and orientation
Development of sentence structure
Understanding purpose of full stops

polar Bear

polar Bears lirk somwe plase
besos it is allwite But somtome
the ice crast then of the polar bear
is ther the polar Bear wil
Flot & wall

Language and Literacy: Writing

Annotation for National Curriculum levels 1C, 1B and 1A

Context

Non-narrative writing task.
'What can we find out about......?' Choice from animal topic.
Pupil worked independently and this work is the first draft.

Evidence

In the reading of his writing John began to show some awareness of how full stops are used.

Performance criteria – Writing

1C Pupils produce recognisable letters and symbols to convey meaning.
Some commonly used letters are correctly shaped but may still be inconsistent in size and orientation.
Some of their writing may still need to be mediated to be understood.

1B Pupils structure some phrases and simple statements using recognisable words to communicate ideas.
Their writing can generally be understood without mediation.
They begin to show an understanding of how full stops are used. Most letters are clearly shaped and correctly orientated.

1A Pupils use phrases and simple statements to convey ideas, making some choices of appropriate vocabulary, and some words are spelt conventionally.
Letters are clearly shaped and correctly orientated. Pupils make some use of full stops and capital letters.

Key elements

Appropriate vocabulary

Next steps

Working on accurate letter formation
Developing sentence structure, focusing on the purpose and use of full stops and capital letters

Monday 16th octobt
my weekend

I went to my friends
house and I had tea
down there house
and I played with clare
and we put on some mousc
there we went home

1A

Language and Literacy: Writing

Annotation for National Curriculum levels 1C, 1B and 1A

Context

Independent writing of weekend news

Evidence

Suzy wrote her weekend news completely unaided.

Performance criteria – Writing

1C Pupils produce recognisable letters and symbols to convey meaning.
Some commonly used letters are correctly shaped but may still be inconsistent in size and orientation.
Some of their writing may still need to be mediated to be understood.

1B Pupils structure some phrases and simple statements using recognisable words to communicate ideas.
Their writing can generally be understood without mediation.
They begin to show an understanding of how full stops are used. Most letters are clearly shaped and correctly orientated.

<u>1A Pupils use phrases and simple statements to convey ideas, making some choices of appropriate vocabulary, and some words are spelt conventionally.</u>
<u>Letters are clearly shaped and correctly orientated. Pupils make some use of full stops and capital letters.</u>

Next steps

Construction of sentences using some appropriate punctuation strategies

Maths: Using and Applying

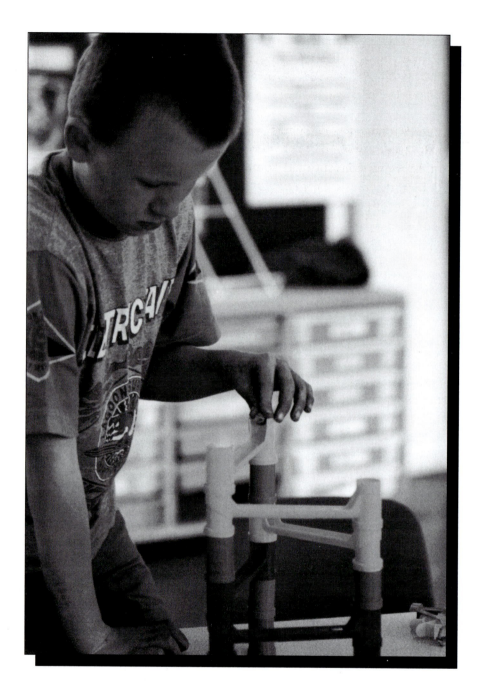

Maths: Using and Applying

Annotation for P levels 3, 4 and 5

Context

Teacher modelled the action of placing a marble in a run and Joe was then asked to copy the action

Evidence

Joe was able to put a marble in the top of the run and clapped when it came out at the bottom.

Performance criteria – Using and Applying

P3(ii) Pupils use emerging conventional communication. They greet known people and may initiate interactions and activities, *for example, dropping objects to prompt interventions from adults.* They can remember learned responses over increasing periods of time and may anticipate known events, *for example, collecting coats and bags at the end of the school day.* They may respond to options and choices with actions or gestures, *for example, pointing to or giving one object rather than another.* They actively explore objects and events for more extended periods, *for example, manipulating objects in piles, groups or stacks.* They apply potential solutions to problems, *for example, using items of equipment purposefully and appropriately.*

<u>P4 **Pupils are aware of cause and effect in familiar mathematical activities**</u>, *for example, hitting a mathematical shape on the concept keyboard to make it appear on the screen.* Pupils show awareness of changes in shape, position or quantity. They anticipate, follow and join in familiar mathematical activities when given a contextual cue.

P5 With support pupils match objects or pictures. They begin to sort sets of objects according to a single attribute. They make sets that have the same number of objects in each. They solve simple problems practically.

Next steps

Generating actions which produce anticipated results

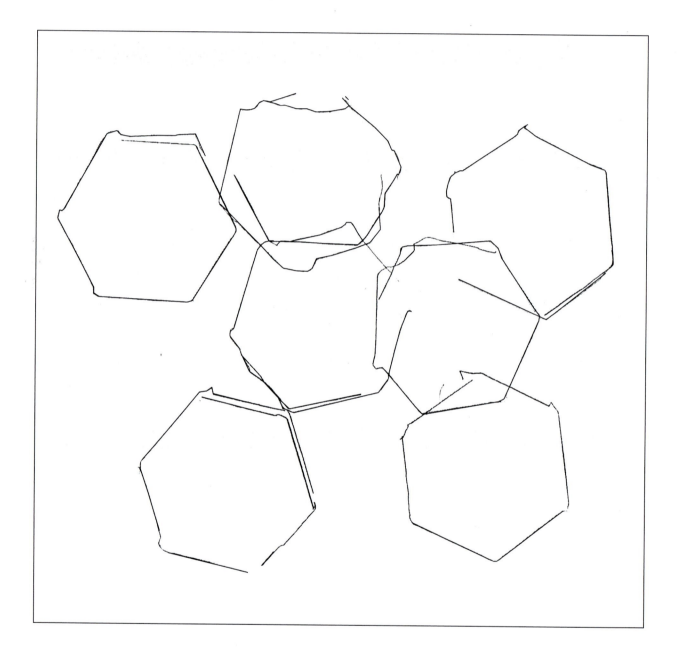

Maths: Using and Applying

Annotation for P levels 4, 5 and 6

Context

Roger was given a set of Logiblocks and asked to find the same shape

Evidence

Roger found another hexagon which was the same. He then picked up a circle, realised it was different and discarded it. He chose to draw round all the hexagons, commenting that they were all the same.

Performance criteria – Using and Applying

P4 Pupils are aware of cause and effect in familiar mathematical activities, *for example, hitting a mathematical shape on the concept keyboard to make it appear on the screen.* Pupils show awareness of changes in shape, position or quantity. They anticipate, follow and join in familiar mathematical activities when given a contextual cue.

P5 With support pupils match objects or pictures. They begin to sort sets of objects according to a single attribute. They make sets that have the same number of objects in each. They solve simple problems practically.

P6 Pupils sort objects and materials according to given criteria. They begin to identify when an object is different and does not belong to given categories. They copy simple patterns or sequences, *for example, a pattern of large and small cups or a drumbeat.*

Next steps

Sorting objects into groups using size
Sorting objects into groups according to size and shape

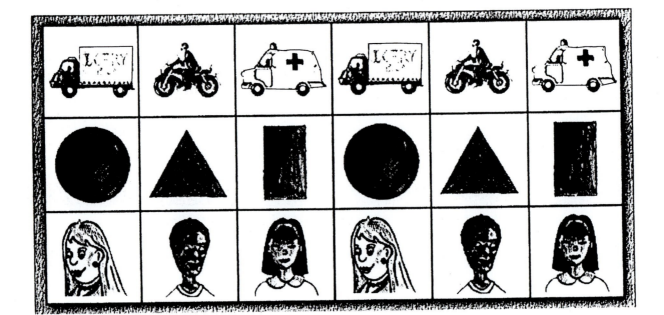

Maths: Using and Applying

Annotation for P levels 5, 6 and 7

Context

Previous work on the computer – making sequences of pictures with help from the teacher. The teacher put a sequence of three pictures on the computer for the pupil to copy.

Evidence

Ruth looked at the set of three the teacher had done and copied the pattern accurately

Performance criteria – Using and Applying

P5 With support pupils match objects or pictures. They begin to sort sets of objects according to a single attribute. They make sets that have the same number of objects in each. They solve simple problems practically.

P6 Pupils sort objects and materials according to given criteria. They begin to identify when an object is different and does not belong to given categories. **They copy simple patterns or sequences,** *for example, a pattern of large and small cups or a drumbeat.*

P7 Pupils complete a range of classification activities using given criteria. They identify when an object is different and does not belong to a given familiar category.

Next steps

Developing sequences independently – initially using real objects, moving on to pictures and/or patterns

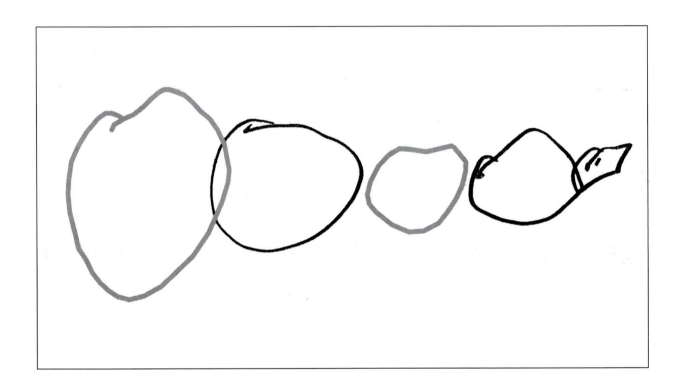

Maths: Using and Applying

Annotation for P levels 6, 7 and 8

Context

Pupils were asked to make a pattern using two colours

Evidence

Virginia made an alternating pattern of circles with blue and yellow crayons.

Performance criteria – Using and Applying

P6 Pupils sort objects and materials according to given criteria. They begin to identify when an object is different and does not belong to given categories. They copy simple patterns or sequences, *for example, a pattern of large and small cups or a drumbeat.*

P7 Pupils complete a range of classification activities using given criteria. They identify when an object is different and does not belong to a given familiar category.

<u>**P8 Pupils**</u> recognise, describe and <u>**recreate simple repeating patterns**</u> and sequences. They begin to use their mathematical understanding of counting to solve simple problems they may encounter in play, games or other work. They begin to make simple estimates, *such as how many cubes will fit in a box.*

Next steps

Recreating patterns with more than one criterion
Developing greater accuracy, e.g. making all the shapes a consistent size

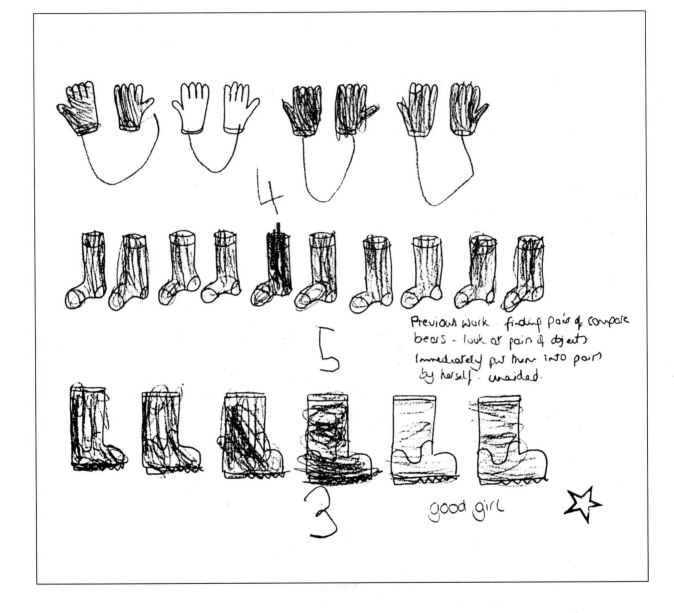

Previous work. finding pairs of compare bears - look at pairs of objects. Immediately put them into pairs by herself. unaided.

good girl

Maths: Using and Applying

Annotation for P levels 7 and 8 and National Curriculum level 1

Context

The task was to make pairs of pictured objects by colouring. Previous work had been done sorting real objects into pairs.

Evidence

Rhiannon coloured pairs of gloves, socks and boots and then independently she counted and recorded how many pairs there were.

Performance criteria – Using and Applying

P7 Pupils complete a range of classification activities using given criteria. They identify when an object is different and does not belong to a given familiar category.

<u>**P8 Pupils recognise, describe and recreate simple repeating patterns and sequences. They begin to use their mathematical understanding of counting to solve simple problems they may encounter in play, games or other work.**</u> They begin to make simple estimates, *such as how many cubes will fit in a box.*

1 Pupils use mathematics as an integral part of classroom activities. They represent their work with objects and pictures and discuss it. They recognise and use a simple pattern or relationship.

Next steps

Opportunities for practical estimation before engaging in activity

Maths: Using and Applying

Annotation for P levels 7 and 8 and National Curriculum level 1

Context

Pupils were each given two Christmas cards which had been cut into pieces. They were asked to sort the cards and reassemble one card.

Evidence

Ripa quickly sorted the cards using the background colour as the main criterion, and then assembled the picture correctly.

Performance criteria – Using and Applying

P7 Pupils complete a range of classification activities using given criteria. They identify when an object is different and does not belong to a given familiar category.

P8 Pupils recognise, describe and recreate simple repeating patterns and sequences. They begin to use their mathematical understanding of counting to solve simple problems they may encounter in play, games or other work. They begin to make simple estimates, *such as how many cubes will fit in a box.*

1 **Pupils use mathematics as an integral part of classroom activities.** They represent their work with objects and pictures and discuss it. **They recognise and use a simple pattern or relationship.**

Next steps

Development of appropriate mathematical language in order to discuss classroom activity

Maths: Number

Maths: Number

Annotation for P levels 3, 4 and 5

Context

Whole-class mental warm up session. Teacher singing the bubble song with children who joined in where they were able.

Evidence

Jerry anticipated the formation of the bubbles at the right time in the song.

Performance criteria – Number (including Handling Data)

<u>P3(ii)</u> <u>Pupils use emerging conventional communication. They greet known people and may initiate interactions and activities.</u> They can remember learned responses over increasing periods of time and may anticipate known events. <u>They may respond to options and choices with actions or gestures.</u> They actively explore objects and events for more extended periods. They apply potential solutions to problems.

<u>P4</u> <u>Pupils show an interest in number activities</u> and counting.

P5 Pupils respond to and join in with familiar number rhymes, songs, stories and games. They can indicate one or two, for example, using their fingers or sounds. They demonstrate that they are aware of contrasting quantities, for example, 'one' and 'lots', by making groups of objects with help.

Next steps

Work towards active involvement, e.g. singing last word, indicating number, using a switch

Maths: Number

Annotation for P levels 4, 5 and 6

Context

1:1 play in the maths session

Evidence

Peter played '2 little dickie birds' with his teacher, holding up and taking away puppets appropriately.

Performance criteria – Number (including Handling Data)

<u>P4 Pupils show an interest in number activities and counting.</u>

<u>P5 Pupils respond to and join in with familiar number rhymes, songs, stories and games.</u>
<u>They can indicate one or two for example, using their fingers</u> or sounds. They demonstrate that they are aware of contrasting quantities, *for example, 'one' and 'lots', by making groups of objects with help.*

<u>P6 Pupils</u> demonstrate their understanding of 1:1 correspondence in a range of contexts. They join in rote counting up to 5 and <u>use numbers to 5 in familiar activities and games.</u>
They count reliably up to 3 objects and make sets of up to 3 objects. They demonstrate an understanding of the concept of more/fewer.
They use 1p coins in shopping for items up to 5p, *for example, in shopping games.*
They join in with new number rhymes, songs, stories and games with some assistance or encouragement.

Next steps

Rote count numbers up to 5
Count objects
Apply understanding to different songs and rhymes

How many in each set?
Draw a ring round the numeral.

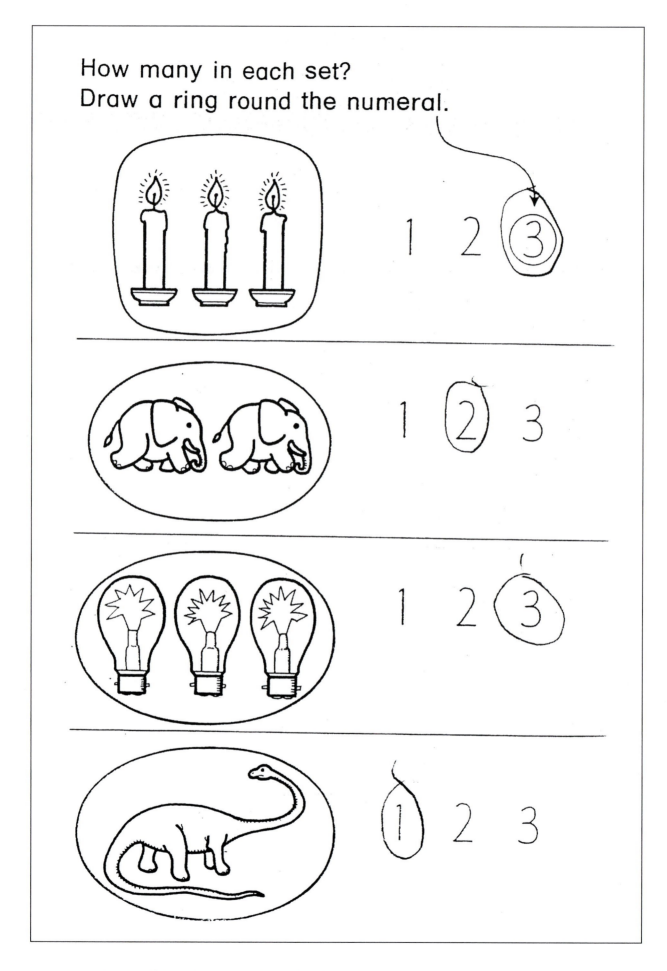

Maths: Number

Annotation for P levels 5, 6 and 7

Context

Counting and recognising numerals

Evidence

John was able to count accurately the given objects and ring the correct numeral independently.

Performance criteria – Number (including Handling Data)

P5 Pupils respond to and join in with familiar number rhymes, songs, stories and games. They can indicate one or two, for example, using their fingers or sounds. They demonstrate that they are aware of contrasting quantities, *for example, 'one' and 'lots', by making groups of objects with help.*

<u>P6 Pupils demonstrate their understanding of 1:1 correspondence</u> in a range of contexts. They join in rote counting up to 5 and <u>use numbers to 5 in familiar activities and games.</u>
<u>They count reliably up to 3 objects and make sets of up to 3 objects. They demonstrate an understanding of the concept of more/fewer.</u>
They use 1p coins in shopping for items up to 5p, *for example, in shopping games*
They join in with new number rhymes, songs, stories and games with some assistance or encouragement.

P7 Pupils join in rote counting to 10. They count reliably at least 5 objects. They begin to recognise numerals from 1 to 5 and to understand that each represents a constant number or amount. They respond appropriately to key vocabulary and questions, for example, *'How many?'* Pupils begin to recognise differences in quantity, *for example, in comparing given sets of objects and saying which has more or less, the bigger group or smaller group.* In practical situations they respond to 'add one' and 'take one'.

Next steps

Counting reliably to 5
Recognise and record numbers to 5

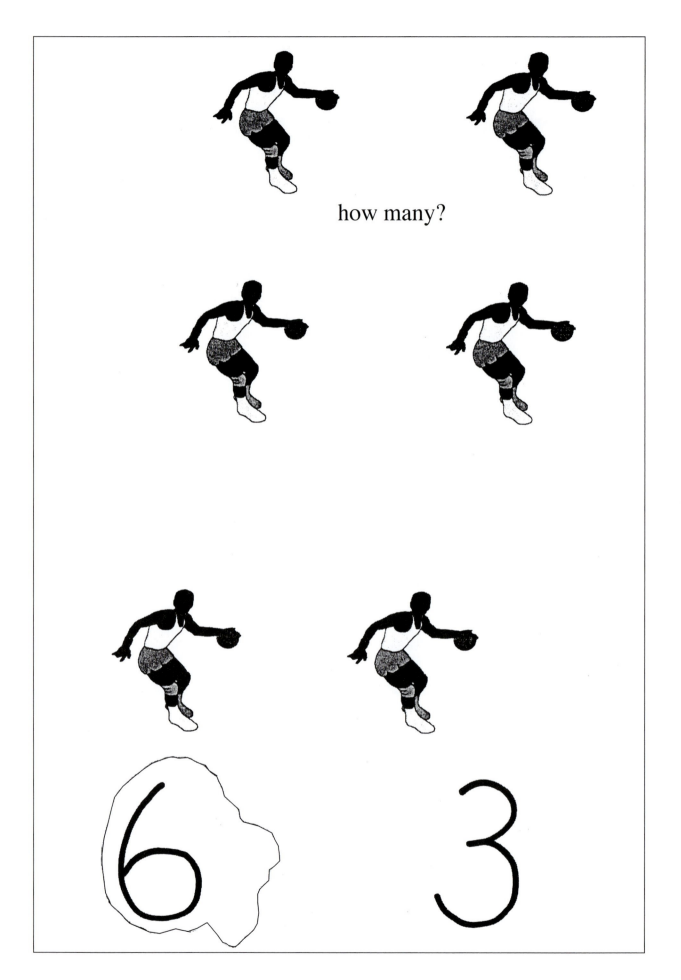

how many?

Maths: Number

Annotation for P levels 6, 7 and 8

Context

Pupils were learning to copy and paste as part of a discrete ICT skills session. They were asked to count how many 'objects' they had produced on their page.

Evidence

Harry accurately counted the objects and chose the correct number from those given by the teacher.

Performance criteria – Number (including Handling Data)

P6 Pupils demonstrate their understanding of 1:1 correspondence in a range of contexts. They join in rote counting up to 5 and use numbers to 5 in familiar activities and games.
They count reliably up to 3 objects and make sets of up to 3 objects. They demonstrate an understanding of the concept of more/fewer.
They use 1p coins in shopping for items up to 5p, *for example, in shopping games*
They join in with new number rhymes, songs, stories and games with some assistance or encouragement.

<u>P7 Pupils join in rote counting to 10. They count reliably at least 5 objects. They begin to recognise numerals from 1 to 5 and to understand that each represents a constant number or amount. They respond appropriately to key vocabulary and questions, for example, 'How many?'</u> Pupils begin to recognise differences in quantity, *for example, in comparing given sets of objects and saying which has more or less, the bigger group or smaller group.* In practical situations they respond to 'add one' and 'take one'.

P8 Pupils join in with rote counting to beyond 10. They continue the rote count onwards from a small given number. They begin to count up to 10 objects . They compare two given numbers of objects saying which is more and which is less. They begin to recognise numerals from 1 to 9 and relate them to sets of objects. In practical situations they add one to or take one away from a number of objects. They begin to use ordinal numbers (first, second, third) when describing positions of objects, people or events. Pupils estimate a small number and check by counting.

Next steps

Identify and read numbers in different contexts

Maths: Number

Annotation for P levels 7 and 8 and National Curriculum level 1C

Context

Teacher working with a small group for counting activity. Estimating and then counting Smarties in a box and comparing amounts with another pupil.

Evidence

Sasha was able to count on accurately from 3. She could say that she had 4 yellow Smarties in her box and that she had more than Mary, who had 3.

Performance criteria – Number (including Handling Data)

P7 Pupils join in rote counting to 10. They count reliably at least 5 objects. They begin to recognise numerals from 1 to 5 and to understand that each represents a constant number or amount. They respond appropriately to key vocabulary and questions, for example, 'How many?' Pupils begin to recognise differences in quantity, *for example, in comparing given sets of objects and saying which has more or less, the bigger group or smaller group.* In practical situations they respond to 'add one' and 'take one'.

P8 Pupils join in with rote counting to beyond 10. They continue the rote count onwards from a small given number. They begin to count up to 10 objects. They compare two given numbers of objects saying which is more and which is less. They begin to recognise numerals from 1 to 9 and relate them to sets of objects. In practical situations they add one to or take one away from a number of objects. They begin to use ordinal numbers (first, second, third) when describing positions of objects, people or events. **Pupils estimate a small number and check by counting.**

1C Pupils read most numerals up to 10 in familiar contexts.
They make attempts to record numbers up to 10.
In practical situations they begin to use vocabulary involved in adding and subtracting and demonstrate an understanding of addition as the combining of two or more groups of objects and subtraction as the taking away of objects from a group.

Next steps

Record numerals up to and including 5
Further opportunities for estimating amounts

1 2 3 4 5 6 7 8 9 10

= 3

= 6

= 2

= 4

= 8

= 11

= 1

Maths: Number

Annotation for P level 8 and National Curriculum levels 1C and 1B

Context

Counting and ordering numbers to 10. Pupils were asked to complete the number line by filling in the missing numbers, and then to count the number of squares given and write the correct numeral after the = sign.

Evidence

The teacher worked with the pupils up to number 3 and Rachel then completed the number lines independently.

She counted and recorded the number squares accurately. When the teacher pointed to the number 7, to indicate that she had written it the wrong way round, Rachel immediately realised her own error and self-corrected it.

She was also able to say which was the biggest and smallest number of squares.

Performance criteria – Number (including Handling Data)

P8 Pupils join in with rote counting to beyond 10. They continue the rote count onwards from a small given number. They begin to count up to 10 objects. They compare two given numbers of objects saying which is more and which is less. They begin to recognise numerals from 1 to 9 and relate them to sets of objects. In practical situations they add one to or take one away from a number of objects. They begin to use ordinal numbers (first, second, third) when describing positions of objects, people or events. Pupils estimate a small number and check by counting.

<u>1C Pupils read most numerals up to 10 in familiar contexts.</u>
<u>They make attempts to record numbers up to 10.</u>
In practical situations they begin to use vocabulary involved in adding and subtracting and demonstrate an understanding of addition as the combining of two or more groups of objects and subtraction as the taking away of objects from a group.

1B Pupils count, read and order numbers up to 10 in a range of settings.
They write numerals up to 10 with increasing accuracy.
Using numbers up to 10, they solve problems involving addition or subtraction, including comparing two sets to find a numerical difference.

Next steps

Adding and subtracting numbers to 10

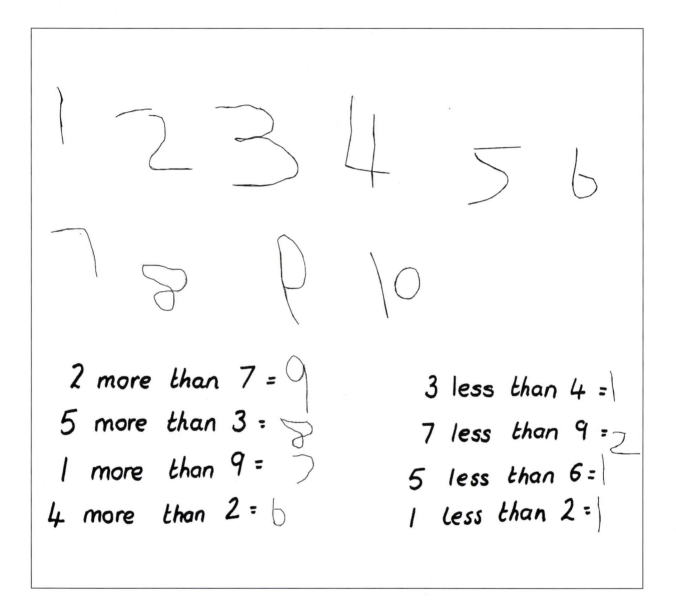

1 2 3 4 5 6
7 8 9 10

2 more than 7 = 9
5 more than 3 = 8
1 more than 9 = 7
4 more than 2 = 6

3 less than 4 = 1
7 less than 9 = 2
5 less than 6 = 1
1 less than 2 = 1

Maths: Number

Annotation for National Curriculum levels 1C, 1B and 1A

Context

Whole-class lesson on ordering numbers to 15 on a number line

Evidence

Rachel worked independently. When given her own set of numbers to 10, Rachel was able to order them correctly. She was able to copy the numbers into her book accurately when asked, and then answered questions relating to these numbers.

Performance criteria – Number (including Handling Data)

1C Pupils read most numerals up to 10 in familiar contexts.
They make attempts to record numbers up to 10.
In practical situations they begin to use vocabulary involved in adding and subtracting and demonstrate an understanding of addition as the combining of two or more groups of objects and subtraction as the taking away of objects from a group.

1B Pupils count, read and order numbers up to 10 in a range of settings.
They write numerals up to 10 with increasing accuracy.
Using numbers up to 10, they solve problems involving addition or subtraction, including comparing two sets to find a numerical difference.

1A Pupils count, read and order numbers from 0 to 20. They write numerals up to 10 and associate these with the number of objects they have counted.
Pupils recognise 0 as 'none' and 'zero' in stories and rhymes and when counting and ordering. They understand operations of addition and subtraction and use related vocabulary. They add and subtract numbers when solving problems involving up to 10 objects in a range of contexts.

Next steps

Ordering numbers to 20
Using addition and subtraction of numbers to 10 in problem solving

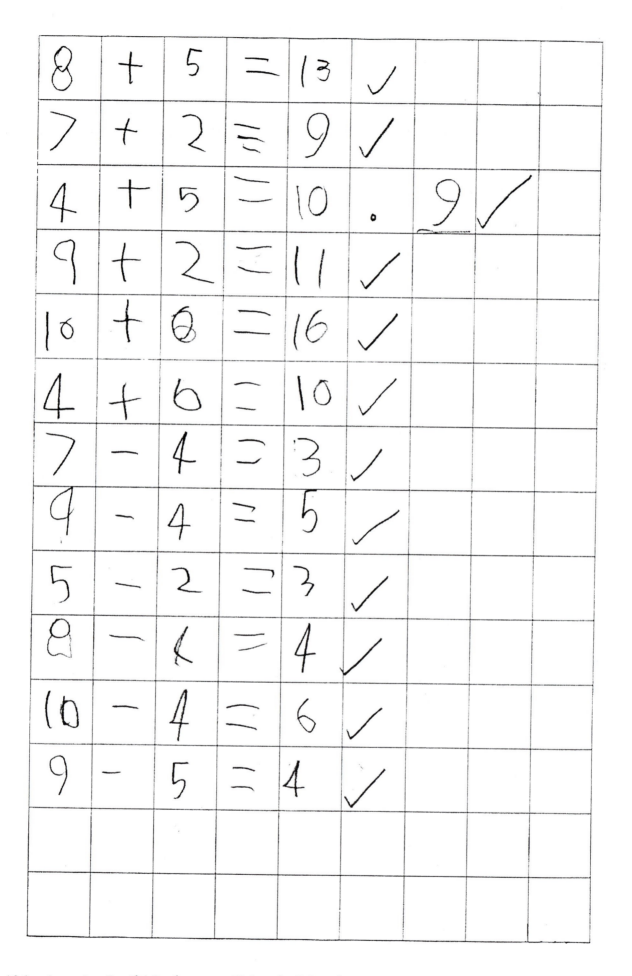

8	+	5	=	13	✓			
7	+	2	=	9	✓			
4	+	5	=	10 .	9 ✓			
9	+	2	=	11	✓			
10	+	8	=	16	✓			
4	+	6	=	10	✓			
7	−	4	=	3	✓			
9	−	4	=	5	✓			
5	−	2	=	3	✓			
8	−	4	=	4	✓			
10	−	4	=	6	✓			
9	−	5	=	4	✓			

Maths: Number

Annotation for National Curriculum levels 1C, 1B and 1A

Context

Whole-class session reading and ordering numbers to 20 using a number line. Following activity: To work independently to add and subtract numbers up to 20, using Multilink to support calculations.

Evidence

Eric was able to count and order numbers independently. He demonstrated his knowledge of number bonds in addition to complete sums and only used Multilink as support when doing subtraction.

Performance criteria – Number (including Handling Data)

1C Pupils read most numerals up to 10 in familiar contexts.
They make attempts to record numbers up to 10.
In practical situations they begin to use vocabulary involved in adding and subtracting and demonstrate an understanding of addition as the combining of two or more groups of objects and subtraction as the taking away of objects from a group.

1B Pupils count, read and order numbers up to 10 in a range of settings.
They write numerals up to 10 with increasing accuracy.
Using numbers up to 10, they solve problems involving addition or subtraction, including comparing two sets to find a numerical difference.

1A <u>Pupils count, read and order numbers from 0 to 20. They write numerals up to 10 and associate these with the number of objects they have counted.</u>
Pupils recognise 0 as 'none' and 'zero' in stories and rhymes and when counting and ordering.
<u>They understand operations of addition and subtraction and use related vocabulary. They add and subtract numbers when solving problems involving up to 10 objects in a range of contexts.</u>

Next steps

Working on understanding of place value up to 20
Using addition and subtraction confidently

Maths: Shape, Space and Measure

Maths: Shape, Space and Measure

Annotation for P levels 3, 4 and 5

Context

Building towers with bricks

Evidence

Steven carefully stacked 5 bricks on top of each other and said, 'My tower is big'.

Performance criteria – Shape, Space and Measure

P3(ii) Pupils use emerging conventional communication. They greet known people and may initiate interactions and activities. They can remember learned responses over increasing periods of time and may anticipate known events. They may respond to options and choices with actions or gestures. They actively explore objects and events for more extended periods. They apply potential solutions to problems.

P4 Pupils begin to search for objects that have gone out of sight, hearing or touch, demonstrating the beginning of object permanence.
They demonstrate interest in position and the relationship between objects, for example, joining in with stacking cups or building towers.

P5 Pupils search intentionally for objects that are in their usual place, for example, going to the mathematics shelf for the box of shapes. They compare the overall size of one object with that of another where there is a marked difference, for example, compare the cup from the doll's house with a breakfast cup and find which is bigger. They find big and small objects on request. They explore the position of objects, for example, putting objects in and out of containers or lining them up.

Next steps

Join shapes and building on horizontally as well as vertically
Begin to compare relative lengths and heights

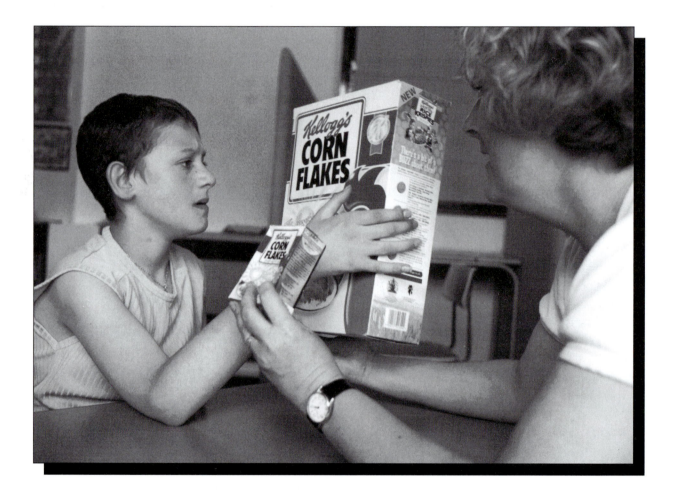

Maths: Shape, Space and Measure

Annotation for P levels 4, 5 and 6

Context

Recognising, sorting, matching, ordering and counting objects
Task was to indicate which were the 'bigger' and 'smaller' cereal packets

Evidence

Leon concentrated intermittently throughout but his attention could be brought back to the task with a single verbal prompt. Leon was able, on several occasions, to point correctly when asked:
'Which is the bigger packet?'
'Which is the smaller packet?'

Performance criteria – Shape, Space and Measure

P4 Pupils begin to search for objects that have gone out of sight, hearing or touch, demonstrating the beginning of object permanence.
They demonstrate interest in position and the relationship between objects, for example, joining in with stacking cups or building towers.

P5 Pupils search intentionally for objects that are in their usual place, for example, going to the mathematics shelf for the box of shapes. **They compare the overall size of one object with that of another where there is a marked difference**, for example, compare the cup from the doll's house with a breakfast cup and find which is bigger. They find big and small objects on request. **They explore the position of objects, for example,** putting objects in and out of containers or **lining them up.**

P6 Pupils search for objects not found in their usual location, demonstrating their understanding of object permanence. They compare the overall size of one object with that of another where the difference is not great, *for example, they find the bigger of two Russian dolls*. They manipulate three-dimensional shapes. They show understanding of words, signs or symbols that describe positions. They use vocabulary such as 'more' or 'less' in practical situations, *for example, they indicate the jug with more juice in it.*

Next steps

Order more than two objects according to size
Order objects using different criteria, e.g. longer/shorter; more/less

Maths: Shape, Space and Measure

Annotation for P levels 5, 6 and 7

Context

Ordering a set of objects. Steven was given a set of bricks and asked to put them in order of size.

Evidence

Steven played with the bricks for a while. He was reminded of the task and he then put the bricks in order. When asked he pointed to 'biggest/smallest' accurately.

Performance criteria – Shape, Space and Measure

P5 Pupils search intentionally for objects that are in their usual place, for example, going to the mathematics shelf for the box of shapes. They compare the overall size of one object with that of another where there is a marked difference, for example, compare the cup from the doll's house with a breakfast cup and find which is bigger. They find big and small objects on request. They explore the position of objects, for example, putting objects in and out of containers or lining them up.

P6 Pupils search for objects not found in their usual location, demonstrating their understanding of object permanence. **They compare the overall size of one object with that of another where the difference is not great**, *for example, they find the bigger of two Russian dolls.* They manipulate three-dimensional shapes. They show understanding of words, signs or symbols that describe positions. They use vocabulary such as 'more' or 'less' in practical situations, *for example, they indicate the jug with more juice in it.*

P7 Pupils begin to respond to forwards and backwards. They start to pick out familiar shapes from a named collection. They use familiar words when they compare sizes and quantities and describe position.

Next steps

Opportunities for further activities involving sorting and ordering using a variety of criteria

Maths: Shape, Space and Measure

Annotation for P levels 6, 7 and 8

Context

Working independently
Sorting shapes

Evidence

Mitchell sorted circles from non-circles using Logiblocks of the same colour.

Performance criteria – Shape, Space and Measure

P6 Pupils search for objects not found in their usual location, demonstrating their understanding of object permanence. They compare the overall size of one object with that of another where the difference is not great, *for example, they find the bigger of two Russian dolls.* They manipulate three-dimensional shapes. They show understanding of words, signs or symbols that describe positions. They use vocabulary such as 'more' or 'less' in practical situations, *for example, they indicate the jug with more juice in it.*

P7 Pupils begin to respond to forwards and backwards. <u>They start to pick out familiar shapes from a named collection.</u> They use familiar words when they compare sizes and quantities and describe position.

P8 Pupils compare directly two lengths or heights where the difference is marked and can indicate 'the long one' or 'the tall one'. They show awareness of time, through familiarity with names of days of week, significant times in their day, for example, meal times, bed time.
They begin to use mathematical vocabulary such as straight, circle, larger to describe shape and size of solids and flat shapes. They describe shapes in simple models, pictures and patterns.

Next steps

Make two sets of shapes from a collection using the same criteria
Name different shapes

THERE WAS AN OLD WOMAN

NUMBER THEME: PATTERN MATCHING

Grouping: Two players.
You will need: An 'old shoe' sheet for each player and a dice with six patterns.

To play:
○ Take turns to throw the dice.
○ Colour in the child which matches the pattern on the dice. If the child is already coloured in, pass the dice on.
○ The winner is the first player to colour all the children.

Maths: Shape, Space and Measure

Annotation for P levels 7 and 8 and National Curriculum level 1C

Context

Matching game as described on the activity sheet

Evidence

Alan was given support to play the game but was not prompted to give answers.
He successfully matched patterns unprompted, and was able to describe the shapes using appropriate language, e.g. circle, square.

Performance criteria – Shape, Space and Measure

P7 Pupils begin to respond to forwards and backwards. <u>They start to pick out familiar shapes from a named collection.</u> They use familiar words when they compare sizes and quantities and describe position.

P8 Pupils compare directly two lengths or heights where the difference is marked and can indicate 'the long one' or 'the tall one'. They show awareness of time, through familiarity with names of days of week, significant times in their day, *for example, meal times, bed time.*
<u>They begin to use mathematical vocabulary such as</u> straight, <u>circle, larger to describe shape</u> and size of solids and <u>flat shapes. They describe shapes in simple</u> models, <u>pictures and patterns</u>.
<u>They use mathematical vocabulary such as</u> *straight, <u>circle</u>, larger* to <u>describe shape</u> and size of solids and <u>flat shapes and use variety of shapes to</u> make and <u>describe</u> simple models, <u>pictures and patterns</u>.

1C Pupils construct with three-dimensional shapes and make patterns and pictures with two-dimensional shapes. They recognise and name some familiar two-dimensional shapes such as circle, triangle, square. They match and sort these shapes in activities.
Beginning to use knowledge of shape to describe properties of everyday objects (e.g. numbers of corners and sides) and to compare them by size.
They use everyday language to describe position, e.g. between, in front of, in the middle, and to compare two quantities, e.g. shorter, heavier.

Next steps

Developing mathematical vocabulary to include solids
Opportunities for constructing models and making pictures and patterns

Classifying

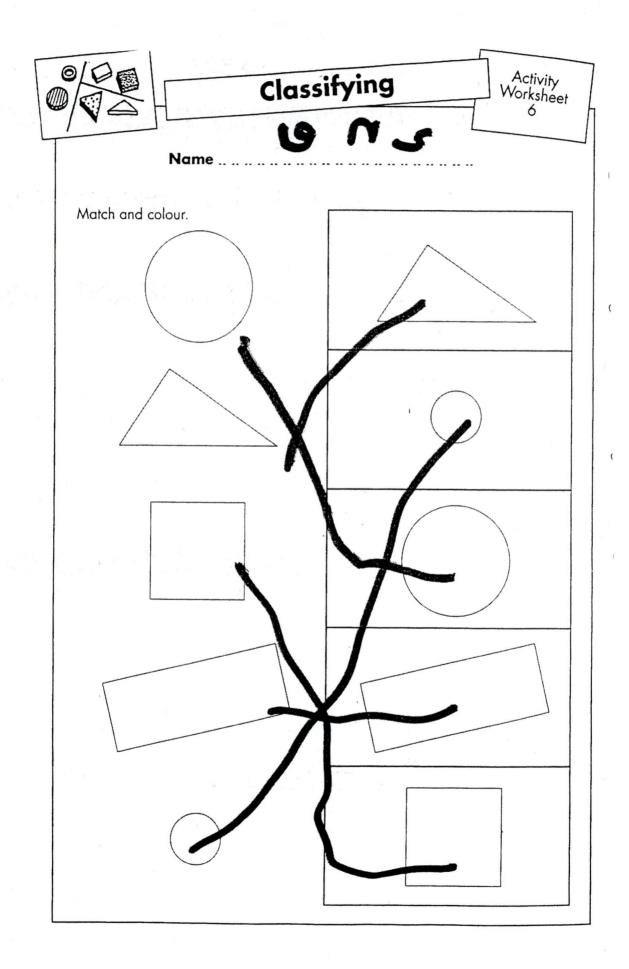

Name ....

Match and colour.

Maths: Shape, Space and Measure

Annotation for P levels 7 and 8 and National Curriculum level 1C

Context

Working independently
Matching shapes

Evidence

David first played with a set of solid shapes.
He then identified the different shapes by name and when given the activity sheet he was able to draw lines to join the shapes which were the same.

Performance criteria – Shape, Space and Measure

P7 Pupils begin to respond to forwards and backwards. They start to pick out familiar shapes from a named collection. They use familiar words when they compare sizes and quantities and describe position.

P8 Pupils compare directly two lengths or heights where the difference is marked and can indicate 'the long one' or 'the tall one'. They show awareness of time, through familiarity with names of days of week, significant times in their day, *for example, meal times, bed time.* **They begin to use mathematical vocabulary *such as straight, circle, larger* to describe shape and size of solids and flat shapes. They describe shapes in simple models, pictures and patterns.**

1C Pupils construct with three-dimensional shapes and make patterns and pictures with two-dimensional shapes. They recognise and name some familiar two-dimensional shapes such as circle, triangle, square. They match and sort these shapes in activities.
Beginning to use knowledge of shape to describe properties of everyday objects (e.g. numbers of corners and sides) and to compare them by size.
They use everyday language to describe position, e.g. between, in front of, in the middle, and to compare two quantities, e.g. shorter, heavier.

Next steps

Develop mathematical vocabulary to describe the properties of objects, e.g. corners; sides
Make patterns with different shapes

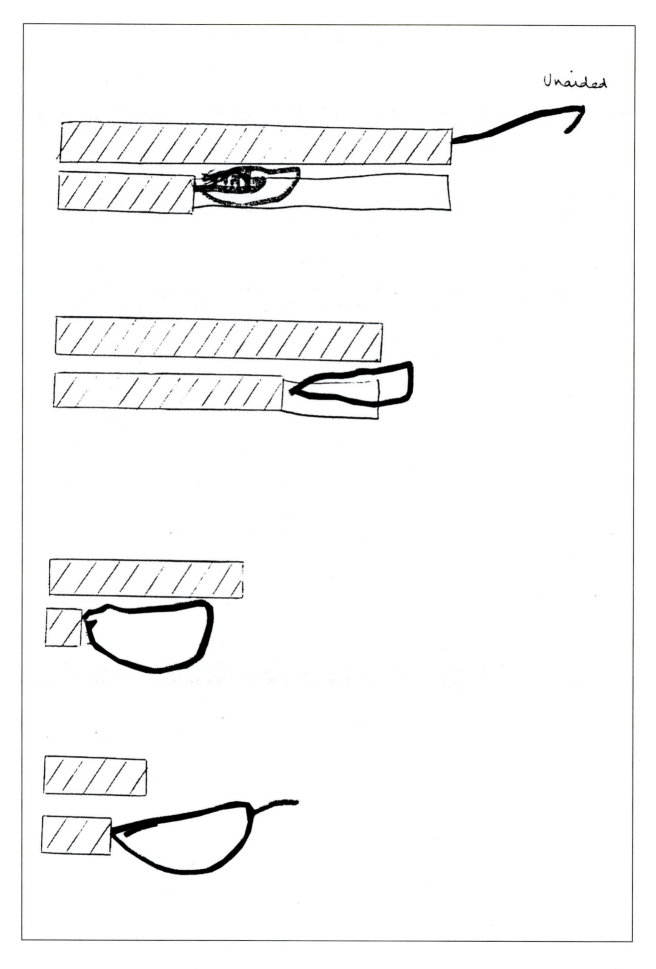

Unaided

Maths: Shape, Space and Measure

Annotation for P levels 7 and 8 and National Curriculum level 1C

Context

Working independently
The task was to make the second rectangle the same length as the first

Evidence

Sam could say which was the longer or shorter.
He drew lines to make the shapes the same length.

Performance criteria – Shape, Space and Measure

P7 Pupils begin to respond to forwards and backwards. They start to pick out familiar shapes from a named collection. They use familiar words when they compare sizes and quantities and describe position.

P8 Pupils **compare directly two lengths** or heights <u>where the difference is marked and can indicate 'the long one'</u> or 'the tall one'. They show awareness of time through familiarity with names of days of week, significant times in their day, *for example, meal times, bed time.*
<u>They begin to use mathematical vocabulary *such as straight, circle, larger* to describe shape and size of solids and flat shapes. They describe shapes in simple models, pictures and patterns.</u>

1C Pupils construct with three-dimensional shapes and make patterns and pictures with two-dimensional shapes. They recognise and name some familiar two-dimensional shapes such as circle, triangle, square. They match and sort these shapes in activities.
Beginning to use knowledge of shape to describe properties of everyday objects (e.g. numbers of corners and sides) and to compare them by size.
They use everyday language to describe position, e.g. between, in front of, in the middle, and to compare two quantities, e.g. shorter, heavier.

Next steps

Focus on pencil control
Explore properties of everyday objects, e.g. shape, size, number of edges

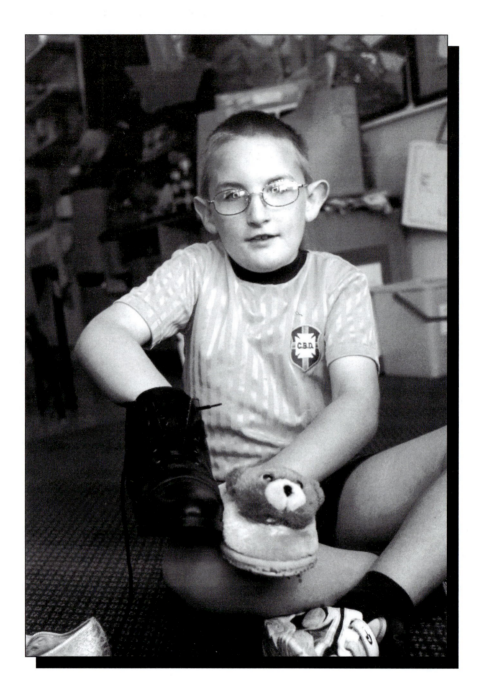

Maths: Shape, Space and Measure

Annotation for P levels 7 and 8 and National Curriculum level 1C

Context

To compare objects of different weights and to say which is heavy and which is light. Check by using a balance.

Evidence

Sean was given a collection of shoes and asked to handle them and pick two shoes and compare them using appropriate mathematical language. He chose two shoes and said one was 'heavy' and one was 'light'. He then put them on a balance to check if he was correct. Using a selection from the collection he was also able to say which was the 'heaviest' and which was the 'lightest'.

Performance criteria – Shape, Space and Measure

P7 Pupils begin to respond to forwards and backwards. They start to pick out familiar shapes from a named collection. They use familiar words when they compare sizes and quantities and describe position.

P8 Pupils compare directly two lengths or heights where the difference is marked and can indicate 'the long one' or 'the tall one'. They show awareness of time, through familiarity with names of days of week, significant times in their day, *for example, meal times, bed time*.
They begin to use mathematical vocabulary *such as straight, circle, larger* to describe shape and size of solids and flat shapes. They describe shapes in simple models, pictures and patterns.

<u>1C</u> Pupils construct with three-dimensional shapes and make patterns and pictures with two-dimensional shapes. They recognise and name some familiar two-dimensional shapes such as circle, triangle, square. They match and sort these shapes in activities.
Beginning to use knowledge of shape to describe properties of everyday objects (e.g. numbers of corners and sides) and to compare them by size.
<u>They use everyday language to</u> describe position, e.g. between, in front of, in the middle, and to <u>compare two quantities, e.g.</u> shorter, <u>heavier</u>.

Next steps

To measure by weight a range of different materials using appropriate mathematical language

Name:_____ Date: 4102.00.

Shapes

Draw a line to link the shape with its name.

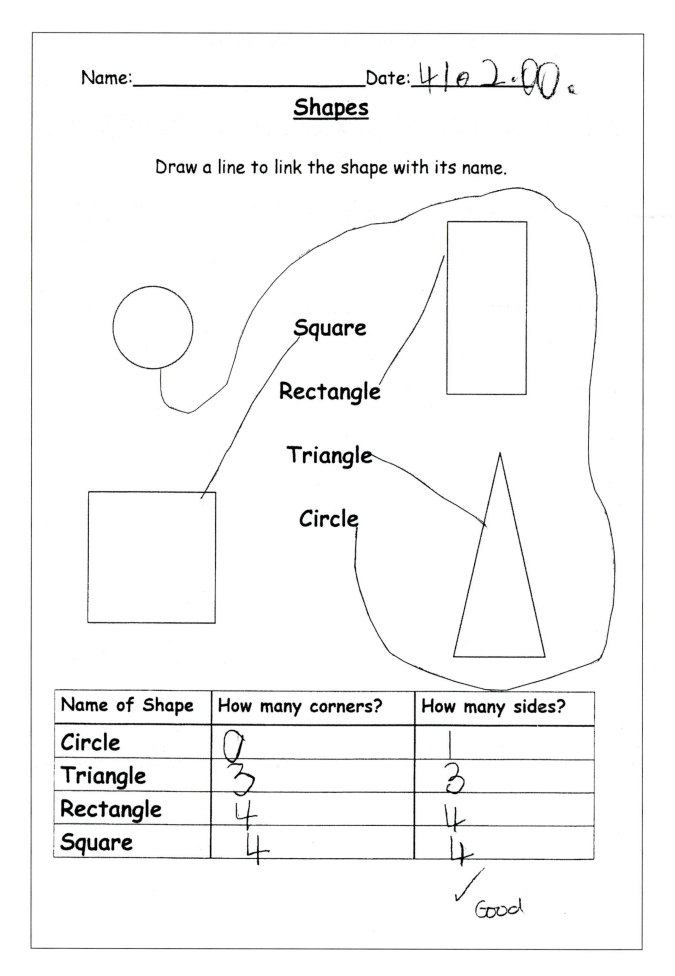

Square

Rectangle

Triangle

Circle

Name of Shape	How many corners?	How many sides?
Circle	0	1
Triangle	3	3
Rectangle	4	4
Square	4	4

✓ Good

Maths: Shape, Space and Measure

Annotation for P level 8 and National Curriculum levels 1C and 1B

Context

After practical whole-group session on 'numbers of sides and corners' pupils were asked to complete activity independently

Evidence

Frank was able to read the words and match them to the correct shape. He showed understanding of the words corners and sides and completed the table accurately.

Performance criteria – Shape, Space and Measure

P8 Pupils compare directly two lengths or heights where the difference is marked and can indicate 'the long one' or 'the tall one'. They show awareness of time, through familiarity with names of days of week, significant times in their day, *for example, meal times, bed time.*
They begin to use mathematical vocabulary *such as straight, circle, larger* to describe shape and size of solids and flat shapes. They describe shapes in simple models, pictures and patterns.

1C Pupils construct with three-dimensional shapes and make patterns and pictures with two-dimensional shapes. <u>They recognise and name some familiar two-dimensional shapes such as circle, triangle, square. They match and sort these shapes in activities.</u>
<u>Beginning to use knowledge of shape to describe properties of everyday objects (e.g. numbers of corners and sides)</u> and to compare them by size.
They use everyday language to describe position, e.g. between, in front of, in the middle, and to compare two quantities, e.g. shorter, heavier.

1B Pupils work with, recognise and name common three-dimensional shapes, e.g. cube, cuboid, sphere, cylinder, and two-dimensional shapes, e.g. circle, triangle, rectangle, square.
They describe basic properties of these shapes and make simple comparisons between them, e.g. larger, smaller, curved, straight. Recognise terms describing position, e.g. behind, in front of, on top. They measure and order more than two objects (by length, mass, capacity) using direct comparison.
They order logically everyday events and begin to use the vocabulary of time.

Next steps

Working with more complex shapes, e.g. hexagons

Maths: Shape, Space and Measure

Annotation for P level 8 and National Curriculum levels 1C and 1B

Context

After discussion and practical session using and naming two-dimensional shapes the task was to draw a picture using different shapes (selecting from square, triangle, rectangle circle, semi-circle).

Each pupil was then asked to identify the shapes they had used and to say how many of each shape.

Evidence

Claire worked independently and completed the task independently.

She said that she had used '14 circles, 2 squares, 2 semi-circles and a lot of rectangles'.

Performance criteria – Shape, Space and Measure

P8 Pupils compare directly two lengths or heights where the difference is marked and can indicate 'the long one' or 'the tall one'. They show awareness of time, through familiarity with names of days of week, significant times in their day, *for example, meal times, bed time.*
They begin to use mathematical vocabulary *such as straight, circle, larger* to describe shape and size of solids and flat shapes. They describe shapes in simple models, pictures and patterns.

1C <u>Pupils</u> construct with three-dimensional shapes and <u>make patterns and pictures with two-dimensional shapes. They recognise and name some familiar two-dimensional shapes such as circle, triangle, square. They match and sort these shapes in activities.</u>
Beginning to use knowledge of shape to describe properties of everyday objects (e.g. numbers of corners and sides) and to compare them by size.
They use everyday language to describe position, e.g. between, in front of, in the middle, and to compare two quantities, e.g. shorter, heavier.

1B <u>Pupils work with, recognise and name common</u> three-dimensional shapes, e.g. cube, cuboid, sphere, cylinder, and <u>two-dimensional shapes, e.g. circle, triangle, rectangle, square.</u>
They describe basic properties of these shapes and make simple comparisons between them, e.g. larger, smaller, curved, straight. Recognise terms describing position, e.g. behind, in front of, on top. They measure and order more than two objects (by length, mass, capacity) using direct comparison.
They order logically everyday events and begin to use the vocabulary of time.

Next steps

Use mathematical language to describe position
Make comparisons by shape, size, etc.

Maths: Shape, Space and Measure

Annotation for National Curriculum levels 1C, 1B and 1A

Context

Pupils were sorting the people in their group in order of size and then to record in pictures. After recording the pupils were asked to match the words to the person.

Evidence

Everyone in the group stood up and Christine started with the teacher as the tallest and moved the group into a line in descending height. She then drew the pictures and copied the words underneath.

Performance criteria – Shape, Space and Measure

1C Pupils construct with three-dimensional shapes and make patterns and pictures with two-dimensional shapes. They recognise and name some familiar two-dimensional shapes such as circle, triangle, square. They match and sort these shapes in activities.
Beginning to use knowledge of shape to describe properties of everyday objects (e.g. numbers of corners and sides) and to compare them by size.
They use everyday language to describe position, e.g. between, in front of, in the middle, and to compare two quantities, e.g. shorter, heavier.

1B Pupils work with, recognise and name common three-dimensional shapes, e.g. cube, cuboid, sphere, cylinder, and two-dimensional shapes, e.g. circle, triangle, rectangle, square.
They describe basic properties of these shapes and make simple comparisons between them, e.g. larger, smaller, curved, straight. Recognise terms describing position, e.g. behind, in front of, on top. **They measure and order more than two objects (by length**, mass, capacity) **using direct comparison**.
They order logically everyday events and begin to use the vocabulary of time.

1A Pupils sort and describe three-dimensional and two-dimensional shapes in terms of their properties and positions. They compare two lengths, masses or capacities by direct comparison. They continue and create simple spatial patterns, e.g. red cylinder, blue cube, red cylinder.... They recognise simple directional symbols such as arrows.

Next steps

To move on to standard measures

Name: _____ Date: 6.6.00.

<u>Repeating patterns.</u>
<u>Continue the patterns of shapes.</u>

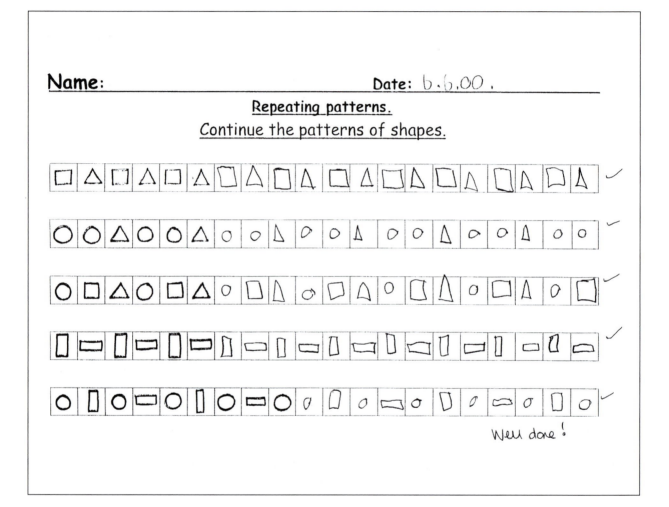

Well done!

Maths: Shape, Space and Measure

Annotation for National Curriculum levels 1C, 1B and 1A

Context

The task was to continue the pattern practically and then record on paper

Evidence

Charlie completed patterns with two and three alternating shapes.

Performance criteria – Shape, Space and Measure

1C Pupils construct with three-dimensional shapes and make patterns and pictures with two-dimensional shapes. They recognise and name some familiar two-dimensional shapes such as circle, triangle, square. They match and sort these shapes in activities.
Beginning to use knowledge of shape to describe properties of everyday objects (e.g. numbers of corners and sides) and to compare them by size.
They use everyday language to describe position, e.g. between, in front of, in the middle, and to compare two quantities, e.g. shorter, heavier.

1B Pupils work with, recognise and name common three-dimensional shapes, e.g. cube, cuboid, sphere, cylinder, and two-dimensional shapes, e.g. circle, triangle, rectangle, square.
They describe basic properties of these shapes and make simple comparisons between them, e.g. larger, smaller, curved, straight. Recognise terms describing position, e.g. behind, in front of, on top. They measure and order more than two objects (by length, mass, capacity) using direct comparison.
They order logically everyday events and begin to use the vocabulary of time.

<u>1A</u> Pupils sort and describe three-dimensional and two-dimensional shapes in terms of their properties and positions. They compare two lengths, masses or capacities by direct comparison.
<u>**They continue and create simple spatial patterns, e.g. red cylinder, blue cube, red cylinder....**</u>
They recognise simple directional symbols such as arrows.

Next steps

Working with patterns using more than one attribute

Annotation sheets – blanks
(Also available from the publisher's website:
www.fultonpublishers.co.uk)

Annotation for P levels 1 to 3

Context

Evidence

Performance criteria

P1(i) Pupils encounter activities and experiences. They may be passive or resistant. They may show simple reflex responses, *for example, starting at sudden noises or movements.* Any participation is fully prompted.

P1(ii) Pupils show emerging awareness of activities and experiences. They may have periods when they appear alert and ready to focus their attention on certain people, events, objects or parts of objects, *for example, starting at sudden noises or movements.* They may give intermittent reactions, *for example, sometimes becoming excited in the midst of social activity.*

P2(i) Pupils begin to respond consistently to familiar people, events and objects. They react to new activities and experiences, *for example, withholding their attention.* They begin to show interest in people, events and objects, *for example, smiling at familiar people.* They accept and engage in coactive exploration, *for example, focusing their attention on sensory aspects of stories or rhymes when prompted.*

Key elements

Next steps

Annotation for P levels 1 to 3

Context

Evidence

Performance criteria

P1(ii) Pupils show emerging awareness of activities and experiences. They may have periods when they appear alert and ready to focus their attention on certain people, events, objects or parts of objects, *for example, grasping objects briefly when they are placed in their hand.* They may give intermittent reactions, *for example, sometimes showing surprise at the sudden presence or absence of an event or object.*

P2(i) Pupils begin to respond consistently to familiar people, events and objects. They react to new activities and experiences, *for example, becoming excited or alarmed when a routine is broken.* They begin to show interest in people, events and objects, *for example, tracking objects briefly across their field of awareness.* They accept and engage in coactive exploration, *for example, lifting objects briefly towards the face in shared investigations.*

P2(ii) Pupils begin to be proactive in their interactions. They communicate consistent preferences and affective responses, *for example, showing a desire to hold a favourite object.* They recognise familiar people, events and objects, *for example, looking towards their own lunch box when offered a selection.* They perform actions, often by trial and improvement, and they remember learned responses over short periods of time, *for example, repeating an action with a familiar item of equipment.* They cooperate with shared exploration and support participation, *for example, handling and feeling the texture of objects passed to them.*

Key elements

Next steps

Annotation for P levels 1 to 3

Context

Evidence

Performance criteria

P2(i) Pupils begin to respond consistently to familiar people, events and objects. They react to new activities and experiences, *for example, withholding their attention*. They begin to show interest in people, events and objects, *for example, smiling at familiar people*. They accept and engage in coactive exploration, *for example, focusing their attention on sensory aspects of stories or rhymes when prompted*.

P2(ii) Pupils begin to be proactive in their interactions. They communicate consistent preferences and affective responses, *for example, reaching out to a favourite person*. They recognise familiar people, events and objects, *for example, vocalising or gesturing in a particular way in response to a favourite visitor*. They perform actions, often by trial and improvement, and they remember learned responses over short periods of time, *for example, showing pleasure each time a particular puppet character appears in a poem dramatised with sensory cues*. They cooperate with shared exploration and support participation, *for example, taking turns in interactions with a familiar person, imitating actions and facial expressions*.

P3(i) Pupils begin to communicate intentionally. They seek attention through eye contact, gesture or action. They request events or activities, *for example, pointing to key objects or people*. They participate in shared activities with less support. They sustain concentration for periods. They explore materials in increasingly complex ways, *for example, reaching out and feeling for objects as tactile cues to events*. They observe the results of their own actions with interest, *for example, listening to their own vocalisations*. They remember learned responses over more extended periods, *for example, following the sequence of a familiar daily routine and responding appropriately*.

Key elements

Next steps

Annotation for P levels 1 to 3

Context

Evidence

Performance criteria

P2(ii) Pupils begin to be proactive in their interactions. They communicate consistent preferences and affective responses, *for example, reaching out to a favourite person.* They recognise familiar people, events and objects, *for example, vocalising or gesturing in a particular way in response to a favourite visitor.* They perform actions, often by trial and improvement, and they remember learned responses over short periods of time, *for example, showing pleasure each time a particular puppet character appears in a poem dramatised with sensory cues.* They cooperate with shared exploration and support participation, *for example, taking turns in interactions with a familiar person, imitating actions and facial expressions.*

P3(i) Pupils begin to communicate intentionally. They seek attention through eye contact, gesture or action. They request events or activities, *for example, pointing to key objects or people.* They participate in shared activities with less support. They sustain concentration for periods. They explore materials in increasingly complex ways, *for example, reaching out and feeling for objects as tactile cues to events.* They observe the results of their own actions with interest, *for example, listening to their own vocalisations.* They remember learned responses over more extended periods, *for example, following the sequence of a familiar daily routine and responding appropriately.*

P3(ii) Pupils use emerging conventional communication. They greet known people and may initiate interactions and activities, *for example, prompting another person to join in with an interactive sequence.* They can remember learned responses over increasing periods of time and may anticipate known events, *for example, pre-empting sounds or actions in familiar poems.* They may respond to options and choices with actions or gestures, *for example, by nodding or shaking their heads.* They actively explore objects and events for more extended periods, *for example, turning the pages in a book shared with another person.* They apply potential solutions systematically to problems, *for example, bringing an object to an adult in order to request a new activity.*

Key elements

Next steps

Language and Literacy: Reading

Annotation for P levels 3, 4 and 5

Context

Evidence

Performance criteria – Reading

P3(ii) Pupils use emerging conventional communication. They greet known people and may initiate interactions and activities, *for example, prompting another person to join in with an interactive sequence.* They can remember learned responses over increasing periods of time and may anticipate known events, *for example, pre-empting sounds or actions in familiar poems.* They may respond to options and choices with actions or gestures, *for example, by nodding or shaking their heads.* They actively explore objects and events for more extended periods, *for example, turning the pages in a book shared with another person.* They apply potential solutions to problems, *for example, bringing an object to an adult in order to request a new activity.*

P4 Pupils listen and respond to familiar rhymes and stories. They show some understanding of how books work, *for example, turning pages and holding the book the right way up.*

P5 Pupils select a few words, signs or symbols with which they are particularly familiar and derive some meaning from text, symbols or signs presented in a way familiar to them. They show curiosity about content at a simple level, *for example, they may answer basic two-word questions about the story.* They match objects to pictures and symbols.

Key elements

Next steps

Language and Literacy: Reading

Annotation for P levels 4, 5 and 6

Context

Evidence

Performance criteria – Reading

P4 Pupils listen and respond to familiar rhymes and stories. They show some understanding of how books work, *for example, turning pages and holding the book the right way up.*

P5 Pupils select a few words, signs or symbols with which they are particularly familiar and derive some meaning from text, symbols or signs presented in a way familiar to them. They show curiosity about content at a simple level, *for example, they may answer basic two-word questions about the story.* They match objects to pictures and symbols.

P6 Pupils select and recognise or read a small number of words or symbols linked to a familiar vocabulary, for example, name, people, objects or actions. They match letters and short words.

Key elements

Next steps

Language and Literacy: Reading

Annotation for P levels 6, 7 and 8

Context

Evidence

Performance criteria – Reading

P6 Pupils select and recognise or read a small number of words or symbols linked to a familiar vocabulary, for example, name, people, objects or actions. They match letters and short words.

P7 Pupils show an interest in the activity of reading. They predict words, signs or symbols in narrative, for example when the adult stops reading, pupils fill in the missing word. They distinguish between print and pictures in texts. They understand the conventions of presentation in their preferred mode of communication, for example, left to right orientation, top to bottom, page following page. They can recognise some letters of the alphabet.

P8 Pupils understand that words, signs, symbols and pictures convey meaning. They read or recognise a growing repertoire of familiar words or symbols, including their own names. They recognise letters of the alphabet by shape, name and sound. They begin to associate sounds with patterns in rhymes, with syllables, and with words, signs, symbols and letters.

Key elements

Next steps

Language and Literacy: Reading

Annotation for P level 8 and National Curriculum levels 1C and 1B

Context

Evidence

Performance criteria – Reading

P8 Pupils understand that words, signs, symbols and pictures convey meaning. They read or recognise a growing repertoire of familiar words or symbols, including their own names. They recognise letters of the alphabet by shape, name and sound. They begin to associate sounds with patterns in rhymes, with syllables, and with words, signs, symbols and letters.

1C Pupils can recognise familiar words, signs, or symbols in simple texts. They identify initial sounds in unfamiliar words. They can establish meaning when reading aloud simple sentences, sometimes with prompting. They express their response to familiar texts by identifying aspects which they like and dislike.

1B Pupils can read a range of familiar words, signs or symbols and identify initial and final sounds in unfamiliar words. With support they use their knowledge of letters, sounds and words to establish meaning when reading aloud. They respond to events and ideas in poems, stories and non-fiction.

Next steps

Language and Literacy: Writing

Annotation for P levels 3, 4 and 5

Context

Evidence

Performance criteria – Writing

P3(ii) Pupils use emerging conventional communication. They greet known people and may initiate interactions and activities, *for example, prompting another person to join in with an interactive sequence*. They can remember learned responses over increasing periods of time and may anticipate known events, *for example, pre-empting sounds or actions in familiar poems*. They may respond to options and choices with actions or gestures, *for example, by nodding or shaking their heads*. They actively explore objects and events for more extended periods, *for example, turning the pages in a book shared with another person*. They apply potential solutions systematically to problems, *for example, bringing an object to an adult in order to request a new activity*.

P4 Pupils begin to understand that marks and symbols convey meaning, *for example, scribbling alongside a picture or placing photographs or symbols on a personal timetable*. They make marks or symbols in their preferred mode of communication, *for example, using writing implements with a pincer grip, generating a symbol from a selection on a computer*.

P5 Pupils produce some meaningful print, signs or symbols associated with their own name or familiar spoken words, actions, images or events, *for example, contributing to records of their own achievements or to books about themselves, their families and interests*. They trace, overwrite and copy under or over a model, making horizontal, vertical and circular lines. With support, they make and complete patterns.

Key elements

Next steps

Language and Literacy: Writing

Annotation for P levels 4, 5 and 6

Context

Evidence

Performance criteria – Writing

P4 Pupils begin to understand that marks and symbols convey meaning, *for example, scribbling alongside a picture or placing photographs or symbols on a personal timetable.* They make marks or symbols in their preferred mode of communication, *for example, using writing implements with a pincer grip, generating a symbol from a selection on a computer.*

P5 Pupils produce some meaningful print, signs or symbols associated with their own name or familiar spoken words, actions, images or events, *for example, contributing to records of their own achievements or to books about themselves, their families and interests.* They trace, overwrite and copy under or over a model, making horizontal, vertical and circular lines. With support, they make and complete patterns.

P6 Pupils differentiate between letters and symbols, *for example, producing a drawing to accompany writing.* They copy writing with support, *for example, labels and/or captions for pictures or for displays.*
They produce or write recognisable letters or symbols related to their names.

Key elements

Next steps

Language and Literacy: Writing

Annotation for P levels 5, 6 and 7

Context

Evidence

Performance criteria – Writing

P5 Pupils produce some meaningful print, signs or symbols associated with their own name or familiar spoken words, actions, images or events, *for example, contributing to records of their own achievements or to books about themselves, their families and interests.* They trace, overwrite and copy under or over a model, making horizontal, vertical and circular lines. With support, they make and complete patterns.

P6 Pupils differentiate between letters and symbols, *for example, producing a drawing to accompany writing.* They copy writing with support, *for example, labels and/or captions for pictures or for displays.*
They produce or write recognisable letters or symbols related to their names.

P7 Pupils group letters and leave spaces between them as though they are writing separate words. Some letters are correctly formed. They are aware of the sequence of letters, symbols and words, *for example, selecting and linking symbols together, writing their own names and one or two other simple words from memory.*

Key elements

Next steps

Language and Literacy: Writing

Annotation for P levels 7 and 8 and National Curriculum level 1C

Context

Evidence

Performance criteria – Writing

P7 Pupils group letters and leave spaces between them as though they are writing separate words. Some letters are correctly formed. They are aware of the sequence of letters, symbols and words, *for example, selecting and linking symbols together, writing their own names and one or two other simple words from memory.*

P8 In their writing and recording pupils use pictures, symbols and familiar words and letters to communicate meaning, showing awareness of the different purposes, *for example, letters, lists, stories or instructions of writing.* They write their names with appropriate use of upper and lower case letters or appropriate symbols.

1C Pupils produce recognisable letters and symbols to convey meaning.
Some commonly used letters are correctly shaped but may still be inconsistent in size and orientation.
Some of their writing may still need to be mediated to be understood.

Key elements

Next steps

Language and Literacy: Writing

Annotation for P level 8 and National Curriculum levels 1C and 1B

Context

Evidence

Performance criteria – Writing

P8 In their writing and recording pupils use pictures, symbols and familiar words and letters to communicate meaning, showing awareness of the different purposes, *for example, letters, lists, stories or instructions of writing.* They write their names with appropriate use of upper and lower case letters or appropriate symbols.

1C Pupils produce recognisable letters and symbols to convey meaning.
Some commonly used letters are correctly shaped but may still be inconsistent in size and orientation.
Some of their writing may still need to be mediated to be understood.

1B Pupils structure some phrases and simple statements using recognisable words to communicate ideas.
Their writing can generally be understood without mediation.
They begin to show an understanding of how full stops are used. Most letters are clearly shaped and correctly orientated.

Key elements

Next steps

Language and Literacy: Writing

Annotation for National Curriculum levels 1C, 1B and 1A

Context

Evidence

Performance criteria – Writing

1C Pupils produce recognisable letters and symbols to convey meaning.
Some commonly used letters are correctly shaped but may still be inconsistent in size and orientation.
Some of their writing may still need to be mediated to be understood.

1B Pupils structure some phrases and simple statements using recognisable words to communicate ideas.
Their writing can generally be understood without mediation.
They begin to show an understanding of how full stops are used. Most letters are clearly shaped and correctly orientated.

1A Pupils use phrases and simple statements to convey ideas, making some choices of appropriate vocabulary and some words are spelt conventionally.
Letters are clearly shaped and correctly orientated. Pupils make some use of full stops and capital letters.

Key elements

Next steps

Maths: Using and Applying

Annotation for P levels 3, 4 and 5

Context

Evidence

Performance criteria – Using and Applying

P3(ii) Pupils use emerging conventional communication. They greet known people and may initiate interactions and activities, *for example, dropping objects to prompt interventions from adults*. They can remember learned responses over increasing periods of time and may anticipate known events, *for example, collecting coats and bags at the end of the school day*. They may respond to options and choices with actions or gestures, *for example, pointing to or giving one object rather than another*. They actively explore objects and events for more extended periods, *for example, manipulating objects in piles, groups or stacks*. They apply potential solutions to problems, *for example, using items of equipment purposefully and appropriately*.

P4 Pupils are aware of cause and effect in familiar mathematical activities, *for example, hitting a mathematical shape on the concept keyboard to make it appear on the screen*. Pupils show awareness of changes in shape, position or quantity. They anticipate, follow and join in familiar mathematical activities when given a contextual cue.

P5 With support pupils match objects or pictures. They begin to sort sets of objects according to a single attribute. They make sets that have the same number of objects in each. They solve simple problems practically.

Next steps

Maths: Using and Applying

Annotation for P levels 4, 5 and 6

Context

Evidence

Performance criteria – Using and Applying

P4 Pupils are aware of cause and effect in familiar mathematical activities, *for example, hitting a mathematical shape on the concept keyboard to make it appear on the screen.* Pupils show awareness of changes in shape, position or quantity. They anticipate, follow and join in familiar mathematical activities when given a contextual cue.

P5 With support pupils match objects or pictures. They begin to sort sets of objects according to a single attribute. They make sets that have the same number of objects in each. They solve simple problems practically.

P6 Pupils sort objects and materials according to given criteria. They begin to identify when an object is different and does not belong to given categories. They copy simple patterns or sequences, *for example, a pattern of large and small cups or a drumbeat.*

Next steps

Maths: Using and Applying

Annotation for P levels 5, 6 and 7

Context

Evidence

Performance criteria – Using and Applying

P5 With support pupils match objects or pictures. They begin to sort sets of objects according to a single attribute. They make sets that have the same number of objects in each. They solve simple problems practically.

P6 Pupils sort objects and materials according to given criteria. They begin to identify when an object is different and does not belong to given categories. They copy simple patterns or sequences, *for example, a pattern of large and small cups or a drumbeat.*

P7 Pupils complete a range of classification activities using given criteria. They identify when an object is different and does not belong to a given familiar category.

Next steps

Assessing Pupils' Performance Using the P Levels © Bristol City Council 2001

Maths: Using and Applying

Annotation for P levels 6, 7 and 8

Context

Evidence

Performance criteria – Using and Applying

P6 Pupils sort objects and materials according to given criteria. They begin to identify when an object is different and does not belong to given categories. They copy simple patterns or sequences, *for example, a pattern of large and small cups or a drumbeat.*

P7 Pupils complete a range of classification activities using given criteria. They identify when an object is different and does not belong to a given familiar category.

P8 Pupils recognise, describe and recreate simple repeating patterns and sequences. They begin to use their mathematical understanding of counting to solve simple problems they may encounter in play, games or other work. They begin to make simple estimates, *such as how many cubes will fit in a box.*

Next steps

Maths: Using and Applying

Annotation for P levels 7 and 8 and National Curriculum level 1

Context

Evidence

Performance criteria – Using and Applying

P7 Pupils complete a range of classification activities using given criteria. They identify when an object is different and does not belong to a given familiar category.

P8 Pupils recognise, describe and recreate simple repeating patterns and sequences. They begin to use their mathematical understanding of counting to solve simple problems they may encounter in play, games or other work. They begin to make simple estimates, *such as how many cubes will fit in a box.*

1 Pupils use mathematics as an integral part of classroom activities. They represent their work with objects and pictures and discuss it. They recognise and use a simple pattern or relationship.

Next steps

Maths: Number

Annotation for P levels 3, 4 and 5

Context

Evidence

Performance criteria – Number (including Handling Data)

P3(ii) Pupils use emerging conventional communication. They greet known people and may initiate interactions and activities. They can remember learned responses over increasing periods of time and may anticipate known events. They may respond to options and choices with actions or gestures. They actively explore objects and events for more extended periods. They apply potential solutions to problems.

P4 Pupils show an interest in number activities and counting.

P5 Pupils respond to and join in with familiar number rhymes, songs, stories and games. They can indicate one or two, for example, using their fingers or sounds. They demonstrate that they are aware of contrasting quantities, for example, 'one' and 'lots', by making groups of objects with help.

Next steps

Maths: Number

Annotation for P levels 4, 5 and 6

Context

Evidence

Performance criteria – Number (including Handling Data)

P4 Pupils show an interest in number activities and counting.

P5 Pupils respond to and join in with familiar number rhymes, songs, stories and games. They can indicate one or two, for example, using their fingers or sounds. They demonstrate that they are aware of contrasting quantities, *for example, 'one' and 'lots', by making groups of objects with help.*

P6 Pupils demonstrate their understanding of 1:1 correspondence in a range of contexts. They join in rote counting up to 5 and use numbers to 5 in familiar activities and games.
They count reliably up to 3 objects and make sets of up to 3 objects. They demonstrate an understanding of the concept of more/fewer.
They use 1p coins in shopping for items up to 5p, *for example, in shopping games.*
They join in with new number rhymes, songs, stories and games with some assistance or encouragement.

Next steps

Maths: Number

Annotation for P levels 5, 6 and 7

Context

Evidence

Performance criteria – Number (including Handling Data)

P5 Pupils respond to and join in with familiar number rhymes, songs, stories and games. They can indicate one or two, for example, using their fingers or sounds. They demonstrate that they are aware of contrasting quantities, *for example, 'one' and 'lots', by making groups of objects with help.*

P6 Pupils demonstrate their understanding of 1:1 correspondence in a range of contexts. They join in rote counting up to 5 and use numbers to 5 in familiar activities and games. They count reliably up to 3 objects and make sets of up to 3 objects. They demonstrate an understanding of the concept of more/fewer. They use 1p coins in shopping for items up to 5p, *for example, in shopping games.* They join in with new number rhymes, songs, stories and games with some assistance or encouragement.

P7 Pupils join in rote counting to 10. They count reliably at least 5 objects. They begin to recognise numerals from 1 to 5 and to understand that each represents a constant number or amount. They respond appropriately to key vocabulary and questions, for example, '*How many?*' Pupils begin to recognise differences in quantity, *for example, in comparing given sets of objects and saying which has more or less, the bigger group or smaller group.* In practical situations they respond to 'add one' and 'take one'.

Next steps

Maths: Number

Annotation for P levels 6, 7 and 8

Context

Evidence

Performance criteria – Number (including Handling Data)

P6 Pupils demonstrate their understanding of 1:1 correspondence in a range of contexts. They join in rote counting up to 5 and use numbers to 5 in familiar activities and games.
They count reliably up to 3 objects and make sets of up to 3 objects. They demonstrate an understanding of the concept of more/fewer.
They use 1p coins in shopping for items up to 5p, *for example, in shopping games.*
They join in with new number rhymes, songs, stories and games with some assistance or encouragement.

P7 Pupils join in rote counting to 10. They count reliably at least 5 objects. They begin to recognise numerals from 1 to 5 and to understand that each represents a constant number or amount. They respond appropriately to key vocabulary and questions, for example '*How many?*' Pupils begin to recognise differences in quantity, *for example, in comparing given sets of objects and saying which has more or less, the bigger group or smaller group.* In practical situations they respond to 'add one' and 'take one'.

P8 Pupils join in with rote counting to beyond 10. They continue the rote count onwards from a small given number. They begin to count up to 10 objects. They compare two given numbers of objects saying which is more and which is less. They begin to recognise numerals from 1 to 9 and relate them to sets of objects. In practical situations they add one to or take one away from a number of objects. They begin to use ordinal numbers (first, second, third) when describing positions of objects, people or events. Pupils estimate a small number and check by counting.

Next steps

Maths: Number

Annotation for P levels 7 and 8 and National Curriculum level 1C

Context

Evidence

Performance criteria – Number (including Handling Data)

P7 Pupils join in rote counting to 10. They count reliably at least 5 objects. They begin to recognise numerals from 1 to 5 and to understand that each represents a constant number or amount. They respond appropriately to key vocabulary and questions, for example, 'How many?' Pupils begin to recognise differences in quantity, *for example, in comparing given sets of objects and saying which has more or less, the bigger group or smaller group.* In practical situations they respond to 'add one' and 'take one'.

P8 Pupils join in with rote counting to beyond 10. They continue the rote count onwards from a small given number. They begin to count up to 10 objects. They compare two given numbers of objects saying which is more and which is less. They begin to recognise numerals from 1 to 9 and relate them to sets of objects. In practical situations they add one to or take one away from a number of objects. They begin to use ordinal numbers (first, second, third) when describing positions of objects, people or events. Pupils estimate a small number and check by counting.

1C Pupils read most numerals up to 10 in familiar contexts.
They make attempts to record numbers up to 10.
In practical situations they begin to use vocabulary involved in adding and subtracting and demonstrate an understanding of addition as the combining of two or more groups of objects and subtraction as the taking away of objects from a group.

Next steps

Maths: Number

Annotation for P level 8 and National Curriculum levels 1C and 1B

Context

Evidence

Performance criteria – Number (including Handling Data)

P8 Pupils join in with rote counting to beyond 10. They continue the rote count onwards from a small given number. They begin to count up to 10 objects. They compare two given numbers of objects saying which is more and which is less. They begin to recognise numerals from 1 to 9 and relate them to sets of objects. In practical situations they add one to or take one away from a number of objects. They begin to use ordinal numbers (first, second, third) when describing positions of objects, people or events. Pupils estimate a small number and check by counting.

1C Pupils read most numerals up to 10 in familiar contexts.
They make attempts to record numbers up to 10.
In practical situations they begin to use vocabulary involved in adding and subtracting and demonstrate an understanding of addition as the combining of two or more groups of objects and subtraction as the taking away of objects from a group.

1B pupils count, read and order numbers up to 10 in a range of settings.
They write numerals up to 10 with increasing accuracy.
Using numbers up to 10, they solve problems involving addition or subtraction, including comparing two sets to find a numerical difference.

Next steps

Maths: Number

Annotation for National Curriculum levels 1C, 1B and 1A

Context

Evidence

Performance criteria – Number (including Handling Data)

1C Pupils read most numerals up to 10 in familiar contexts.

They make attempts to record numbers up to 10.

In practical situations they begin to use vocabulary involved in adding and subtracting and demonstrate an understanding of addition as the combining of two or more groups of objects and subtraction as the taking away of objects from a group.

1B Pupils count, read and order numbers up to 10 in a range of settings.

They write numerals up to 10 with increasing accuracy.

Using numbers up to 10, they solve problems involving addition or subtraction, including comparing two sets to find a numerical difference.

1A Pupils count, read and order numbers from 0 to 20. They write numerals up to 10 and associate these with the number of objects they have counted.

Pupils recognise 0 as 'none' and 'zero' in stories and rhymes and when counting and ordering. They understand operations of addition and subtraction and use related vocabulary. They add and subtract numbers when solving problems involving up to 10 objects in a range of contexts.

Next steps

Maths: Shape, Space and Measure

Annotation for P levels 3, 4 and 5

Context

Evidence

Performance criteria – Shape, Space and Measure

P3(ii) Pupils use emerging conventional communication. They greet known people and may initiate interactions and activities. They can remember learned responses over increasing periods of time and may anticipate known events. They may respond to options and choices with actions or gestures. They actively explore objects and events for more extended periods. They apply potential solutions to problems.

P4 Pupils begin to search for objects that have gone out of sight, hearing or touch, demonstrating the beginning of object permanence.
They demonstrate interest in position and the relationship between objects, for example, joining in with stacking cups or building towers.

P5 Pupils search intentionally for objects that are in their usual place, for example, going to the mathematics shelf for the box of shapes. They compare the overall size of one object with that of another where there is a marked difference, for example, compare the cup from the doll's house with a breakfast cup and find which is bigger. They find big and small objects on request. They explore the position of objects, for example, putting objects in and out of containers or lining them up.

Next steps

Maths: Shape, Space and Measure

Annotation for P levels 4, 5 and 6

Context

Evidence

Performance criteria – Shape, Space and Measure

P4 Pupils begin to search for objects that have gone out of sight, hearing or touch, demonstrating the beginning of object permanence.
They demonstrate interest in position and the relationship between objects, for example, joining in with stacking cups or building towers.

P5 Pupils search intentionally for objects that are in their usual place, for example, going to the mathematics shelf for the box of shapes. They compare the overall size of one object with that of another where there is a marked difference, for example, compare the cup from the doll's house with a breakfast cup and find which is bigger. They find big and small objects on request. They explore the position of objects, for example, putting objects in and out of containers or lining them up.

P6 Pupils search for objects not found in their usual location, demonstrating their understanding of object permanence. They compare the overall size of one object with that of another where the difference is not great, *for example, they find the bigger of two Russian dolls*. They manipulate three-dimensional shapes. They show understanding of words, signs or symbols that describe positions. They use vocabulary such as 'more' or 'less', in practical situations, *for example, they indicate the jug with more juice in it*.

Next steps

Maths: Shape, Space and Measure

Annotation for P levels 5, 6 and 7

Context

Evidence

Performance criteria – Shape, Space and Measure

P5 Pupils search intentionally for objects that are in their usual place, for example, going to the mathematics shelf for the box of shapes. They compare the overall size of one object with that of another where there is a marked difference, for example, compare the cup from the doll's house with a breakfast cup and find which is bigger. They find big and small objects on request. They explore the position of objects, for example, putting objects in and out of containers or lining them up.

P6 Pupils search for objects not found in their usual location, demonstrating their understanding of object permanence. They compare the overall size of one object with that of another where the difference is not great, *for example, they find the bigger of two Russian dolls*. They manipulate three-dimensional shapes. They show understanding of words, signs or symbols that describe positions. They use vocabulary such as 'more' or 'less', in practical situations, *for example, they indicate the jug with more juice in it*.

P7 Pupils begin to respond to forwards and backwards. They start to pick out familiar shapes from a named collection. They use familiar words when they compare sizes and quantities and describe position.

Next steps

Maths: Shape, Space and Measure

Annotation for P levels 6, 7 and 8

Context

Evidence

Performance criteria – Shape, Space and Measure

P6 Pupils search for objects not found in their usual location, demonstrating their understanding of object permanence. They compare the overall size of one object with that of another where the difference is not great, *for example, they find the bigger of two Russian dolls*. They manipulate three-dimensional shapes. They show understanding of words, signs or symbols that describe positions. They use vocabulary such as 'more' or 'less', in practical situations, *for example, they indicate the jug with more juice in it*.

P7 Pupils begin to respond to forwards and backwards. They start to pick out familiar shapes from a named collection. They use familiar words when they compare sizes and quantities and describe position.

P8 Pupils compare directly two lengths or heights where the difference is marked and can indicate 'the long one' or 'the tall one'. They show awareness of time, through familiarity with names of days of week, significant times in their day, *for example, meal times, bed time*.
They begin to use mathematical vocabulary such as straight, circle, larger to describe shape and size of solids and flat shapes. They describe shapes in simple models, pictures and patterns.

Next steps

Maths: Shape, Space and Measure

Annotation for P levels 7 and 8 and National Curriculum level 1C

Context

Evidence

Performance criteria – Shape, Space and Measure

P7 Pupils begin to respond to forwards and backwards. They start to pick out familiar shapes from a named collection. They use familiar words when they compare sizes and quantities and describe position.

P8 Pupils compare directly two lengths or heights where the difference is marked and can indicate 'the long one' or 'the tall one'. They show awareness of time, through familiarity with names of days of week, significant times in their day, *for example, meal times, bed time.*
They begin to use mathematical vocabulary such as straight, circle, larger to describe shape and size of solids and flat shapes. They describe shapes in simple models, pictures and patterns.
They use mathematical vocabulary such as *straight, circle, larger* to describe shape and size of solids and flat shapes and use variety of shapes to make and describe simple models, pictures and patterns.

1C Pupils construct with three-dimensional shapes and make patterns and pictures with two-dimensional shapes. They recognise and name some familiar two-dimensional shapes such as circle, triangle, square. They match and sort these shapes in activities.
Beginning to use knowledge of shape to describe properties of everyday objects (e.g. numbers of corners and sides) and to compare them by size.
They use everyday language to describe position, e.g. between, in front of, in the middle, and to compare two quantities, e.g. shorter, heavier.

Next steps

Maths: Shape, Space and Measure

Annotation for P level 8 and National Curriculum levels 1C and 1B

Context

Evidence

Performance criteria – Shape, Space and Measure

P8 Pupils compare directly two lengths or heights where the difference is marked and can indicate 'the long one' or 'the tall one'. They show awareness of time, through familiarity with names of days of week, significant times in their day, *for example, meal times, bed time.*
They begin to use mathematical vocabulary *such as straight, circle, larger* to describe shape and size of solids and flat shapes. They describe shapes in simple models, pictures and patterns.

1C Pupils construct with three-dimensional shapes and make patterns and pictures with two-dimensional shapes. They recognise and name some familiar two-dimensional shapes such as circle, triangle, square. They match and sort these shapes in activities.
Beginning to use knowledge of shape to describe properties of everyday objects (e.g. numbers of corners and sides) and to compare them by size.
They use everyday language to describe position, e.g. between, in front of, in the middle, and to compare two quantities, e.g. shorter, heavier.

1B Pupils work with recognise and name common three-dimensional shapes, e.g. cube, cuboid, sphere, cylinder, and two-dimensional shapes, e.g. circle, triangle, rectangle, square.
They describe basic properties of these shapes and make simple comparisons between them, e.g. larger, smaller, curved, straight. Recognise terms describing position, e.g. behind, in front of, on top. They measure and order more than two objects (by length, mass, capacity) using direct comparison.
They order logically everyday events and begin to use the vocabulary of time.

Next steps

Maths: Shape, Space and Measure

Annotation for National Curriculum levels 1C, 1B and 1A

Context

Evidence

Performance criteria – Shape, Space and Measure

1C Pupils construct with three-dimensional shapes and make patterns and pictures with two-dimensional shapes. They recognise and name some familiar two-dimensional shapes such as circle, triangle, square. They match and sort these shapes in activities.

Beginning to use knowledge of shape to describe properties of everyday objects (e.g. numbers of corners and sides) and to compare them by size.

They use everyday language to describe position, e.g. between, in front of, in the middle, and to compare two quantities, e.g. shorter, heavier.

1B Pupils work with, recognise and name common three-dimensional shapes, e.g. cube, cuboid, sphere, cylinder, and two-dimensional shapes, e.g. circle, triangle, rectangle, square.

They describe basic properties of these shapes and make simple comparisons between them, e.g. larger, smaller, curved, straight. Recognise terms describing position, e.g. behind, in front of, on top. They measure and order more than two objects (by length, mass, capacity) using direct comparison.

They order logically everyday events and begin to use the vocabulary of time.

1A Pupils sort and describe three-dimensional and two-dimensional shapes in terms of their properties and positions. They compare two lengths, masses or capacities by direct comparison. They continue and create simple spatial patterns, e.g. red cylinder, blue cube, red cylinder.... They recognise simple directional symbols such as arrows.

Next steps